D0031219

Daily Inspiration for

FINDING
FAVOR *with the*
KING

TOMMY
TENNEY

Books by Tommy Tenney

GOD CHASERS SERIES
The God Chasers
God's Favorite House
The God Catchers
God's Eye View
Prayers of a God Chaser
(Study guides and workbooks are
available for many of these books)

UNITY SERIES
God's Dream Team
Answering God's Prayer
God's Secret to Greatness

COMPASSION SERIES
Chasing God, Serving Man
Mary's Prayers and Martha's Recipes

FAMILY SERIES
How to Be a God Chaser and a Kid Chaser
On Daddy's Shoulders

DEVOTIONAL BOOKS
The Daily Chase
Experiencing His Presence
Up Where You Belong

GIFT BOOKS
Heart of a God Chaser
God Chasers for Kids
God Chasers for Teens
You Are a God Chaser If. . .

OTHER BOOKS
Trust and Tragedy
Secret Sources of Power
Finding Favor With the King

FICTION
The Ultimate Comeback
Hadassah: One Night With the King
Hadassah: The Girl Who Became Queen Esther
The Hadassah Covenant

TOMMY TENNEY

DAILY INSPIRATION FOR

FINDING FAVOR with the KING

BETHANYHOUSE

MINNEAPOLIS, MINNESOTA

Published by Bethany House Publishers
11400 Hampshire Avenue South
Bloomington, Minnesota 55438

Bethany House Publishers is a division of
Baker Publishing Group, Grand Rapids, Michigan.

Printed in the United States of America

ISBN-13:   978-0-7642-0308-4
ISBN-10:   0-7642-0308-8

Library of Congress Cataloging-in-Publication Data

Tenney, Tommy, 1956–
    Daily inspiration for finding favor with the King : 90 devotional readings / Tommy
Tenney.
        p.   cm.
    Summary: "A 90-day devotional based on 'Finding Favor With the King.' Provides
instruction on how to prepare for a meeting with the divine King by using parallels from the
life of Esther and King Xerxes (500 BC)"—Provided by publisher.
    ISBN-13: 978-0-7642-0308-4 (hardcover : alk. paper)
    ISBN-10: 0-7642-0308-8 (hardcover : alk. paper)
 1. Bible. O.T. Esther—Devotional use. I. Title.
    BS1375.54.T46   2006
    242'.5—dc22   2006019511

Dedication

To the "Esthers" who would learn.

About the Author

TOMMY TENNEY is known for his passionate pursuit of God's presence, a passion that birthed bestselling books such as *The God Chasers* and *Finding Favor With the King*.

Readers worldwide have validated Tommy's fresh approach of relating to God. His books have been published in over forty languages and have sold more than five million copies in English. Daily e-mail devotionals by Tommy are received by hundreds of thousands, and the GodChasers.net Web site is viewed over one million times per month. His casual but relevant television programs are broadcast from many networks and into more than one hundred twenty nations.

With a recent venture into fiction, Tommy retells the ancient story of Esther in a two-part series, *Hadassah: One Night With the King*, and its contemporary sequel, *The Hadassah Covenant*. The *One Night With the King* novel has been made into a major motion picture, with actors such as Peter O'Toole and Omar Sharif.

While being passionate after God, Tommy has great compassion for man. His thirty-plus years in ministry include ten years leading a local church. He considers himself a world citizen and multifaceted minister. Having ministered in more than fifty nations and thousands of local churches, he has recently spent considerable time and resources in the devastated hurricane areas. As a Louisiana resident, he has been particularly involved in the restoration of New Orleans.

While these passions drive Tommy, his family sustains him. His wife, three daughters, two Yorkies, one son-in-law (and two grandchildren to date!) are a constant source of joy.

Acknowledgments

Many thanks to
Larry Walker, Kyle Duncan, Gary and Carol Johnson,
and the whole Baker/Bethany team.

Table of Contents

Day One

RUN TO DADDY

*Some forms of worship only release their sweetest fragrance
to God when offered from the fires of trial and adversity.*
Finding Favor With the King, 25

SCRIPTURE READING

ACTS 16:25–34, WHERE PAUL AND SILAS, BEATEN AND
LOCKED UP IN THE PHILIPPIAN JAIL, OFFERED PRAYER AND
PRAISE TO GOD, WHO DELIVERED THEM WITH AN
EARTHQUAKE, AFTER WHICH THE JAILER AND HIS ENTIRE
HOUSEHOLD BECAME BELIEVERS.

A mentality is afoot in some sectors of the church today that
teaches believers to expect an easy road in life. "Just have faith
and everything will be fine!" If you're sick, struggling with your finances,
or having problems on the job or in relationships, it's because you don't
have enough faith. Christians are overcomers. Life should be a breeze!

There's one thing wrong with this attitude: *it flies in the face of reality.*
Christians go bankrupt. Christians get cancer. Christians lose their jobs.
Trials and adversity are real, even for believers. They touch every one of
us, and they hurt. And they usually have nothing to do with our faith
level.

How do you handle adversity in your life? Do you gripe and complain about your lot? "Oh, woe is me!" Do you challenge or question God? "Why are you letting this happen to me?" Or do you view trials as an opportunity to grow and draw closer to your heavenly Father?

Children who get a cut or a scrape run to Mommy or Daddy for comfort and the kiss that will make it all better. Love is given and received, and bonds deepen between parent and child during such times.

In the same way, trials and hard times should propel us into our Father's arms, not cause us to run the other way. Faith is one thing, expecting faith to shelter us from all difficulty and hardship is another. It just won't happen. Jesus, in fact, told us the opposite: "If the world hates you, you know that it hated Me before it hated you. . . . Remember the word that I said to you, 'A servant is not greater than his master.' If they persecuted Me, they will also persecute you."[1] However, He also tempered this grim news with a great promise: "In the world you will have tribulation; but be of good cheer, I have overcome the world."[2]

Trials and adversity are part of life in a fallen world, particularly for Christians because we are on assignment in enemy territory. They are the purifying flames that our loving Father will use to cleanse us, burn away all our impurities, and shape and strengthen us for service in His name—*if we will let Him.* The trials of life can either make us or break us, depending on our response.

When Paul and Silas languished in that prison in Philippi, their feet tight in the stocks and their backs bruised and bleeding from their beatings, they could have moaned and groaned about the unfairness of life. Instead, at midnight they were "praying and singing hymns to God."[3] They turned their pain into praise and their sores into songs of joy. In the midst of tribulation their jubilant worship went up as a sweet fragrance of faith and love, and the Father's deliverance came down and literally shook the earth. The fragrance of their worship permeated those around them, including the jailer and his family, and changed their lives forever.

---

[1]John 15:18, 20a.
[2]John 16:33b.
[3]Acts 16:25a.

Athletes understand the truth of "no pain, no gain." They know that in order to grow stronger their muscles must be stressed and stretched to the painful breaking point in exercise so new tissue will generate. We cannot grow without pain and resistance. It's a fact of life. God uses our trials and hardships to draw us to Him, to bring us to maturity, and to prepare us for greater things. Our willing worship in times of tribulation is a sweet fragrance to God that brings Him near.

It's easy to praise God when things are going well. When was the last time you worshiped Him during hard times? Try viewing your trials and adversity as opportunities for praise, worship, and growth. When life hurts, don't run away—*run to Daddy*!

PRAYER

Father, sometimes life hurts, and my first impulse is to turn my back or run away. I know You love me and I know that You want to use even the bad times and the sad times to draw me to Your side and make me more like You. I'm sorry for worshiping You only when things are going well. Teach me to worship You at all times, and let my worship be a sweet fragrance rising to Your throne.

PERSONAL REFLECTIONS

Day Two

BE PREPARED

Protocol of the Palace #1
Never underestimate the potential of one encounter.
Finding Favor With the King, 26

SCRIPTURE READING

ACTS 8:26–39, IN WHICH AN ETHIOPIAN GOVERNMENT
OFFICIAL, RETURNING HOME FROM WORSHIPING IN
JERUSALEM AND READING SCRIPTURE ALONG THE WAY, HAS
AN ENCOUNTER WITH PHILIP—A DIVINE APPOINTMENT
THAT CHANGES HIS DESTINY AND, QUITE POSSIBLY, THAT
OF HIS PEOPLE.

First impressions are lasting impressions. You only have one chance to make a good first impression, so prepare yourself.

How do you prepare for a job interview? A major project at work? A big presentation at school? A first date? How would you dress? How would you act? How would you approach important events such as these? Would you do your best to ensure that every detail and element was in place, or would you try to "wing it"?

Nobody likes to be embarrassed or humiliated. We all try to be on our best behavior for significant events in our lives. Just as no one with good sense would go to a job interview or on a first date "winging it," so too no one goes in to see a king unprepared.

Esther prepared herself *intensively* for an entire year before her encounter with the king. To do otherwise would have been disastrous. One slipup, one error in protocol, would have meant losing her life. Had that happened, she never would have fulfilled her destiny and delivered her people. Of course, at the time, Esther had no idea of the role she would play or the divine appointment that lay ahead for her. Nevertheless, she prepared herself carefully and diligently. She did not underestimate the potential of her one encounter with the king.

Those of us who live in democratic societies have trouble understanding the protocols of royalty because the concept is foreign to us. Yet the protocols for meeting modern heads of state are similar in many ways. In the summer of 2005, a university national champion women's lacrosse team had the honor of meeting President Bush in the White House and having their picture taken with him. A minor controversy of sorts arose over the fact that four of the women wore flip-flops to the meeting. Comments from several quarters suggested that flip-flops were inappropriate footwear for a meeting with the president.

Whatever your personal take on the "flip-flop flap," the fact remains that certain protocols apply when meeting people in authority, particularly heads of state. *Why are preparation and protocol so important? Because you never know beforehand the result, outcome, or consequences of a single meeting.*

The Ethiopian official on his way home from Jerusalem had no idea how that one encounter was about to change his life. But he was prepared for it nevertheless, even though he did not know what was coming. First, he had *worshiped* God in Jerusalem. Now, on his way home, he was reading the Scriptures. Specifically, he was reading the book of Isaiah and trying to understand it. He found favor with God who, drawn by his honest and earnest seeker's heart, sent Philip to explain the gospel to him.

This Ethiopian's encounter with Philip lasted a matter of hours at most, perhaps only a matter of minutes. Yet that one encounter changed his destiny because in that encounter he met Jesus Christ. More than that, his encounter very likely had a profound influence on the spiritual destiny of his people. Ethiopia has a Christian tradition that stretches back almost two thousand years. Many scholars believe this tradition began with this one official who met Philip on the road that day.

Life is full of strategic encounters and divine appointments. The problem is that so many of us miss them when they come because we are not expecting or looking for them. We are not prepared when they happen.

Why risk squandering a once-in-a-lifetime opportunity by being too lazy or too shortsighted to prepare? You never know how one encounter with the right person may change your life. On the other hand, you never know how a person's encounter with *you* may change that person's life. It cuts both ways.

Never underestimate the potential of one encounter. Don't take the events and seeming coincidences of life for granted. Prepare for your future by immersing yourself now in the fragrant aromas of worship, prayer, and careful attention to God's Word. This will sensitize you to the strategic encounters and divine appointments that God brings into your life. *Be prepared!*

===

PRAYER

Father, forgive me for missing strategic encounters because I wasn't ready. Forgive me for taking You for granted or presuming upon Your love for me. Help me prepare through worship, prayer, and Your Word to see Your activity in my life. Prepare me also to be Your instrument in strategic encounters that will change others' lives.

Day Three

WHAT DO YOU WANT?

Whatever impresses you attracts you.
Whatever you pursue becomes your purpose.
Finding Favor With the King, 28

===

SCRIPTURE READING

MATTHEW 6:19–21; 31–33, IN WHICH JESUS CAUTIONS HIS
LISTENERS NOT TO FOCUS ON TEMPORARY RICHES ON
EARTH BUT ON ETERNAL RICHES IN HEAVEN; NOT TO
WORRY ABOUT DAILY NEEDS BUT FOCUS ON SEEKING
THE KINGDOM OF GOD.

===

H*e who dies with the most toys—**still dies.***
What do you want out of life? What inspires you? What attracts you? What is the driving force that gets you up and going every day? What are you living for? Family? Fame? Money? Honor? A nicer car? A bigger house? Or are you living for the honor and glory of the King of Kings?

The Great Pyramid of Giza near Cairo in Egypt, one of the seven wonders of the ancient world, still impresses people today with the immensity of its mass and the precision of its construction. Built over forty-five hundred years ago by the Fourth Dynasty pharaoh Khufu to serve as his personal tomb, the Great Pyramid remained the tallest man-made structure in the world until the nineteenth century.

The opulence of these Egyptian tombs was legendary. Gold, jewels, and other priceless treasures of all kinds were buried with the pharaohs to ease their passage into the afterlife and provide for their needs after they arrived there. Khufu's pyramid was the greatest of all of these tombs, so when the first (supposedly) explorers dug their way painstakingly into the tomb centuries after its construction, they expected to find literally a "king's ransom" of wealth. What they actually found was— *nothing*. No gold, no jewels, no precious treasures of any kind. Even the mummy case containing the embalmed body of Khufu was gone. Unknown grave robbers had long since stripped the burial chamber bare. Nothing remained except the red granite sarcophagus. Khufu died and could not take his wealth with him. Instead, anonymous thieves took it *from* him! And what was left? A massive outwardly impressive tomb for a dead king whose body had long since turned to dust.

Most people today spend their lives chasing things that do not last. They consume their best and most productive years in the pursuit of wealth, pleasure, and fame—which are as fleeting as the wind—and reach the end of their lives with nothing to show for all their labor.

What good are riches, possessions, or fame without spiritual wealth? What's the use of accumulating things *here* if you have nothing waiting in the *hereafter*? After all, you will never see a hearse pulling a U-Haul. The writer of Ecclesiastes said, "As he came from his mother's womb, naked shall he return, to go as he came; and he shall take nothing from his labor which he may carry away in his hand."[1] Jesus said, "For what profit is it to a man if he gains the whole world, and loses his own soul? Or what will a man give in exchange for his soul?"[2]

Most people have it backwards. They pursue things and possessions, expecting to build security for themselves and their families. But they

[1]Ecclesiastes 5:15.
[2]Matthew 16:26.

have no wealth of spirit. They are like the man Jesus described who built bigger barns to hold all his grain so he could relax in luxury. But when God required an accounting of his soul, he was not ready.[3]

True security is found in seeking the kingdom of God. Seek the things of the Spirit and everything else will be supplied. Be careful about what you allow to impress you. Whatever *impresses* you will *attract* you. A strong enough attraction will draw you into pursuit. And whatever you pursue becomes your purpose.

Pursue the King and He becomes your purpose. When you pursue the King, you gain His kingdom *and everything that goes with it.* This is why Jesus said, "Seek first the kingdom of God and His righteousness, and all these things shall be added to you."[4] When you pursue the King, He will give you everything else you need.

Jim Elliot, a missionary who was martyred in the jungles of South America in 1956, said: "He is no fool who gives what he cannot keep to gain what he cannot lose."[5] The choice is yours. You can spend your life pursuing things of the world that will pass away. Or you can spend your life in pursuit of the King and His kingdom, which will never pass away. What will be your purpose in life? *What do you want?*

═══

PRAYER

Father, it's so easy to get caught up in following the world and going after the things the world values. Without You, those things mean nothing. Apart from You they are worthless. I want You more than anything this world has to offer. Whatever I pursue becomes my purpose. I want to pursue You, Your kingdom, and Your righteousness. And I will trust You for everything else I need.

---

[3]Luke 12:16–21.
[4]Matthew 6:33.
[5]Elisabeth Elliot, *Through Gates of Splendor* (Wheaton, IL: Tyndale House, 1986).

Day Four

BREAD? OR THE BREAD-GIVER?

Protocol of the Palace #2
Seek the heart of the King,
not the splendor of His kingdom.
Finding Favor With the King, 31

═══

SCRIPTURE READING

JOHN 6:26–29, IN WHICH JESUS, THE DAY AFTER FEEDING
THE FIVE THOUSAND, CHALLENGES THE PEOPLE TO SEEK
HIM, NOT BECAUSE HE GAVE THEM ORDINARY BREAD BUT
BECAUSE HE CAN GIVE THEM *LIVING* BREAD—HIMSELF.

═══

What does it mean to pursue the King?

For one thing, it means wanting to *know Him*, not just hang around Him.

Have you ever seen people whose sole purpose in life seems to be staying as close as possible to someone of power, authority, or influence? Their only interest seems to be in what *they can get* from their association with this person. They couldn't care less about really *knowing* the person. Their only concern is the prestige they have in being able to say, "I'm on the inside track" or "I'm in the loop."

Like every other leader in history, Jesus had His share of "hangers-on." He was surrounded by people who followed Him because of what they thought He could *do for* them. They didn't really care who He was; all they were interested in was what they could get from Him.

Jesus even had to deal with this attitude within His own inner circle. One day James and his brother John, the "sons of thunder,"[1] brazenly asked Jesus for the privilege of sitting on His right and left hand in glory. This made the other disciples angry. (Probably because they hadn't thought of it first!) Jesus used this occasion to teach them that the measure of true greatness in the kingdom of God is seen in a heart and attitude of *servanthood.*[2]

People who are always jockeying for position aren't interested in serving but in being served. Christians who do this reveal that they really know nothing of the *heart* of the King. Jesus said, "For even the Son of Man did not come to be served, but to serve, and to give His life a ransom for many."[3]

In John 6:26–29 it is the day after Jesus fed five thousand people with five loaves of bread and two fish. The same crowd has followed Him to Capernaum, on the other side of the Sea of Galilee. There Jesus confronts them about their attitude. "You seek Me, not because you saw the signs, but because you ate of the loaves and were filled. Do not labor for the food which perishes, but for the food which endures to everlasting life, which the Son of Man will give you."[4]

A lot of these folks were hanging around Jesus, not because they loved Him or believed in Him as the Messiah but because they wanted another free meal! They wanted to see Him do more amazing things. They wanted to bask in the aura of His popularity so they could say to an "outsider," "I'm with *Him!*"

In the verses that follow, Jesus refers to Himself as the "Bread of Life" and removes all illusions about what it means to be "with Him."

---

[1]Mark 3:17.
[2]Mark 10:35–45.
[3]Mark 10:45.
[4]John 6:26b–27a.

It is not a free ride or a free lunch but a life of faith and commitment to Him that leads to everlasting life. This is not what the crowd wants to hear: "From that time many of His disciples went back and walked with Him no more."[5] All they wanted was free bread. They weren't interested in knowing the Bread-Giver. They were hanging on for the splendor of the free ride, and when its luster faded so did they.

If you're serious about pursuing the King, you will seek to *know* Him. You will seek His *heart.* You will love Him for *who He is*, not for what He has done or may do for you. You will seek to think as He thinks, love as He loves, and do as He does. You will hang on His every word out of the sheer joy of simply being *with* Him! When you are with the King, nothing else matters!

Are you seeking the *heart* of the King or just the splendor of His kingdom? Do you want Him for who He is or for what He can do for you? Here's one way to tell. Think about this: *If you lost everything and all you had left was your relationship with the King, would that be enough?* Would you be satisfied?

What are you after? Bread? Or the *Bread-Giver?*

===

PRAYER

Lord, I want to know Your heart! I want to know Your mind. I want to feel as You feel, think as You think, and love as You love. Help me look beyond Your gifts and Your blessings and the splendor of Your kingdom so I can see You! As long as I can be with You and know You, nothing else matters!

---

[5]John 6:66.

Day Five

PRESS IN DEEPER

Protocol of the Palace #3
One day of favor can be worth
more than a lifetime of labor!
Finding Favor With the King, 36

≡

SCRIPTURE READING

PSALM 30, IN WHICH DAVID EXTOLS THE LORD FOR
HIS FAVOR, WHICH LASTS FOR A LIFETIME AND BY
WHICH DAVID'S KINGDOM STANDS STRONG AND
IS FIRMLY ESTABLISHED.

≡

W*ould you do me a favor?"*
How often does someone ask this of you? How often does the request come from your own lips? In one form or another, most of us hear this request almost every day. The very form of the question tells us a lot about *favor*. Asking someone for a favor is a request based not on merit but on *relationship*. We ask not because we have "earned" the right but on the basis of some relationship that exists between us and the person of whom we make the request. That relationship gives us confidence that our request likely will be granted.

In the Bible, another word for favor is *grace*. In fact, grace is often defined as "God's unmerited *favor*." God gives His grace freely to all who ask in faith. When we come to Him in repentance, He forgives us of our sins and accepts us into His kingdom. He does this not because we deserve it or have earned it but because He *chooses to do so*. This is God's favor.

Most people in the world who practice any kind of religious belief or ritual spend their lives working to *earn* the favor of their "god," however they perceive him. Unfortunately, there are many who go by the name *Christian* who have fallen into the same trap. Here's the problem: We cannot *earn* God's favor. He must *give* it. And even then, *it is at His sole discretion.*

A lifetime of religious "labor" may yield legalism and self-righteous religious pride but little else. The apostle Paul wrote, "For by grace you have been saved through faith, and that not of yourselves; it is the gift of God, *not of works*, lest anyone should boast."[1] The Pharisees and other Jewish religious leaders of Jesus' day thought they were God's "favorites" because of their rigorous attention to the letter of the Law. What God wanted all along was for them to *seek His heart*. But their hearts were far away from Him. As long as they were satisfied in their own self-righteousness they would never know the true favor of God.

David, Israel's greatest king, knew that his success was not due to his own merit or goodness but to God's favor. In Psalm 30 he wrote: "For His anger is but for a moment, His favor is for life; weeping may endure for a night, but joy comes in the morning. Now in my prosperity I said, 'I shall never be moved.' Lord, by Your favor You have made my mountain stand strong."[2]

Favor trumps works. One of the most beautiful examples in the Bible of God's favor is the story of Joseph in the book of Genesis. Sold into slavery by his jealous brothers, Joseph served ably and with integrity in the household of Potiphar, the pharaoh's captain of the guard. Later, falsely accused of rape, Joseph spent several years in prison. All this time,

---

[1]Ephesians 2:8–9, emphasis added.
[2]Psalm 30:5–7a.

however, God was preparing Joseph for his moment. When Joseph's day came, he found favor in the eyes of the pharaoh (as well as in the eyes of God, his heavenly King). In a *moment* Joseph was transformed from slave and prison inmate to Pharaoh's second-in-command. For Joseph, one day of favor was worth more than a lifetime of labor. Joseph easily could have spent the rest of his life laboring faithfully—and remained a slave. God's favor was upon him, however, and that made all the difference. God honored Joseph's faithfulness, but in the end it was God's *favor*, not Joseph's labor, that elevated him.

God's grace is His unmerited favor freely given to all who ask. There is also, however, a deeper level of God's favor that is more selective. It cannot be earned but is available to anyone who will "pay the price" to walk the extra mile or go to the extra "trouble" to *seek and know the heart of God.* God extends His grace for salvation to all who receive Him. The privilege of *pressing in to know God's heart begins with another choice.* It is an invitation open to everyone.

As a Christian, you don't have to *earn* God's favor—you already have it! You are a beneficiary of His grace—His unmerited favor *freely given.* And He loves you with an everlasting love.[3] Greater favor and deeper intimacy with Him await you if you will make it your goal to press in and *pursue the heart of God* rather than simply enjoying the benefits of His grace. *Press in deeper!*

═════

PRAYER

Lord, thank You for Your grace, Your unmerited favor by which I have been saved and forgiven. Thank You for loving me with an everlasting love. I want to press in deeper with You. I want to go beyond simply enjoying the benefits of Your grace. I want to press in until I know Your very heart. Draw me close, Father, even as I seek to draw near.

---

[3]Jeremiah 31:3.

Day Six

BE ALL THAT YOU CAN BE

You are chosen for potential but kept because of passion.
Finding Favor With the King, 37

===

SCRIPTURE READING

FIRST PETER 2:9–10, WHICH TELLS HOW GOD
CHOSE US OUT OF THE DARKNESS OF SIN TO BE HIS
SPECIAL PEOPLE: A CHOSEN GENERATION, A ROYAL
PRIESTHOOD, AND A HOLY NATION.

===

Everybody has potential.

Within each of us lies the possibilities of either the heights of success or the depths of failure. We each possess the potential for the greatest good or the greatest evil. That is how God created us. Fortunately for all of us, failure does not disqualify us from enjoying the love and favor of God.

One of the consequences of God's grace and favor is that our continuing fellowship with God is based on *relationship* and not on anything we do or fail to do. In one way or another all of us have failed to fulfill our God-given potential. But isn't it wonderful to know that God never gives up on us? He keeps right on working patiently with us, picking us up when we fall, kissing our skinned knees and elbows, and lovingly helping us to try again. As our loving heavenly Father, His heart's desire is to see every one of us become everything He created us to be. He wants to see us reach our potential.

But our relationship with God does not stand or fall based on how well we succeed. There is no minimum standard of "performance" we must meet in order to gain His approval and acceptance. God already accepts us on the basis of what His Son, Jesus, did on the cross. The cross demonstrated God's love and acceptance of us beyond any doubt. Paul stated it this way: "But God demonstrates His own love toward us, in that while we were still sinners, Christ died for us."[1]

God knows our potential but keeps us close because of His passionate love for us. *He loves us so much that He can't stand to have us out of His sight!*

So often we fail to realize our full potential because we don't really know who we are in Christ. We don't understand the full range of what God has placed within us. As a race we have been falling short of our potential ever since Adam and Eve came up short in the garden of Eden. The story of the entire Bible is the record of God's plan and effort to reverse that failure.

Look what God has done for us. First Peter 2:9–10 tells us that God has transformed us from people of darkness to people of "His marvelous light." We who were not a people are now the "people of God." We are "a chosen generation, a royal priesthood, a holy nation, *His own special people.*"[2]

After Adam and Eve's failure in Eden, God could have written us off and started over. But He didn't. He loved us. He created us in His image. That's a lot of potential, and He is determined to see us fulfill it.

What dreams and desires for your life has God planted in your heart? He wants to see you achieve them or He wouldn't have placed them there. As He did with Esther, God has a unique and special destiny for

[1]Romans 5:8.
[2]1 Peter 2:9a, emphasis added.

you; a plan to give you "a future and a hope."[3] He has something in mind that only you can do. It doesn't matter how many times you may have failed. It doesn't matter how many wrong choices you may have made along the way. God's plan and dream for you—your destiny—will never change. And no matter where you are in your life, He can help you become what He has always wanted you to be.

God chose you for the potential He placed in you, but He keeps you because of His passion for you. This means He will never abandon you. He will never give up on you. He will never rest until He elevates you into the fullness of the person He created you to be.

Sound scary? Take heart from this promise: "'You are My servant, I have chosen you and have not cast you away: Fear not, for I am with you; be not dismayed, for I am your God. I will strengthen you, yes, I will help you, I will uphold you with My righteous right hand.'"[4]

God chose you for potential but keeps you because of passion. Don't settle for less than the best. *Be all that you can be!*

═══

PRAYER

Father, I am truly amazed at how You can love me so passionately, especially when I've failed you and let you down so many times. I don't want to settle for less than the best. Show me who I truly am in You. Stir in my spirit the dream and destiny You have planted there. Help me move toward becoming all I can be in You.

---

[3]Jeremiah 29:11b.
[4]Isaiah 41:9b–10.

Day Seven

THE KING'S HOME IS YOUR HEART

*The King's palace without the King
is just a big empty house.*
Finding Favor With the King, 38

===

SCRIPTURE READING

MARK 13:1–2, WHERE ONE OF JESUS' DISCIPLES REMARKS ON
THE MAGNIFICENCE OF THE TEMPLE AND JESUS FORETELLS
ITS COMPLETE DESTRUCTION.

===

Jesus' announcement that the temple in Jerusalem would be destroyed prompted a lengthy discussion about the signs of the end of the age. In the minds of Jesus' disciples, nothing could be more cataclysmic to their world than the destruction of the temple. This just goes to show that looks can be deceiving. Sometimes we are too easily impressed by the wrong things. God looks at things much differently than we do.

The temple that Jesus and His disciples knew was a grand enlargement and renovation of the second temple that had been built under Ezra's leadership after the Babylonian exile. Herod the Great, who died c. 4 BC, began the project to please his Jewish subjects. His expansion plan was so grand in scale that renovations and new construction were not completed until 66 AD. Four years later, this grand temple was destroyed by the Romans, along with the entire city of Jerusalem—just as Jesus had foretold. Some semblance of its magnificence can still be seen in the massive stones of its only surviving remnant—the Western Wall (or "Wailing Wall") at the temple mount in Jerusalem.

Like the second temple it was based on, the Most Holy Place in Herod's temple had no ark of the covenant. For centuries the ark had represented to the Jews the literal presence of God in the temple. After the days of Judas Maccabeus the temple gradually became more of a political institution than a house of worship and prayer. The office of high priest became a hereditary political position.

Great and impressive rituals and formal observances took place at the temple every day. But few of those involved were aware that the Master of the house was not in residence. We gain some sense of the spirit of the place in the gospel accounts of Jesus driving out the money-changers for turning the "house of prayer" into a "den of thieves."[1]

We must come to realize the same truth that the disciples had to learn: *The presence of the King is not found in buildings of stone and mortar but in the hearts of His children!* Paul said, "God, who made the world and everything in it, since He is Lord of heaven and earth, does not dwell in temples made with hands."[2] The important thing is not the building or its luxurious and elegant trappings. The important thing is the presence of the King. It is the presence of the King that makes the house a palace. Apart from His presence, the house might as well be a shack. In fact, even the simplest, shabbiest, drabbest shack becomes a beautiful palace if the presence of the King is there.

The *true* palace of the King is wherever the King is in residence. As Christians, each of us is the King's palace because He resides in us through the Holy Spirit. Paul says that our bodies are temples of the Holy Spirit who lives in us.[3] In this sense at least, we take the King with

---

[1]Matthew 21:13; Mark 11:17; Luke 19:46.
[2]Acts 17:24.
[3]1 Corinthians 6:19.

us wherever we go. This is the difference between being the King's concubine and being His *bride*. As I wrote in *Finding Favor With the King*, "Concubines may have had an *experience* with the King. His bride would *have* the King!" (38).

As Christians, we do not simply *experience* the King. We *have* the King as a living daily presence within us! We are His holy bride! *And no matter where we are, we are in a palace, because we are with Him!*

=====

PRAYER

Lord, my King, You have shared many great and wonderful gifts with me. But the greatest gift of all is the gift of Yourself. Thank You for Your constant, daily, abiding presence in my life. Help me live each day in such a way that others will see the splendor and glory of Your presence shining through me.

PERSONAL REFLECTIONS

Day Eight

INTIMATE BUT NOT FAMILIAR

You cannot worship what you dethrone!
Finding Favor With the King, 41

═══

SCRIPTURE READING

ISAIAH 6:1–8, WHERE THE PROPHET IN A VISION
SEES THE KING, THE LORD OF HOSTS, ON HIS THRONE
AND IS OVERCOME WITH REVERENCE AND HOLY
FEAR AT THE SIGHT.

═══

I *ntimacy does not necessarily mean familiarity.*
Those closest to the King will never presume familiarity with Him. Instead, they will exalt, honor, revere, and worship Him more than those who are farther away. Why? Because *the King's intimates know Him for who He really is. And that knowledge leaves them awestruck!*

Worship fosters intimacy. But those who *truly* worship *never* take their intimacy with the King lightly. Even Esther did not presume to approach King Xerxes uninvited or unannounced. She could have been executed. This is why her decision to go to him on behalf of her threatened people was such a courageous act. Esther understood the awesome power and authority of her husband. She willingly risked her own life and future to intercede for her people.

Parents and children share an intimate relationship. Yet at the same time a certain "distance" exists between them. I love it when my daughters call me "Daddy." No one else in the world but them have that privilege. My girls enjoy an exclusive relationship with me. Yet that title *Daddy* preserves a certain distance between us. They are my daughters; I am their father. They are intimate with me, but not familiar the way my wife is.

In the same way, God loves us and invites us into intimacy with Him. But there will always be a certain distance between Him and us. After all, He is God and we are not. The more intimate we become with the King, the less familiar we will be with Him. We will better understand the reverence, awe, and worship that are due Him.

This is exactly what Isaiah discovered. Isaiah honored and worshiped God. But it took a vision of the Lord on His throne for Isaiah to see Him as He truly is. And that vision overwhelmed him. In a moment Isaiah's perspective on everything changed. He saw God's power and majesty and glory and holiness. His response? *He worshiped.*

You cannot worship what you dethrone. The old saying "Familiarity breeds contempt" is very true. The more we get to know someone, the more flaws we see. Familiarity cuts the lofty down to size. It takes a person off the pedestal in our eyes.

Some churches and Christians assume a casual familiarity toward God that is completely unbiblical. Those who appear the most familiar with God are actually the least intimate with Him. Their very familiarity reveals that their view of God is too small and limited. Otherwise they would know better.

As children of God we have the right to be intimate with Him. At the same time, however, there is a definite and infinite "otherness" about God that is utterly supernatural. And that otherness deserves our honor, our respect, our reverence, and our worship. The King invites you into His inner chamber. Go ahead! Be intimate! *Just don't be familiar!*

═══

PRAYER

Father, thank You for inviting me to be intimate with You. Forgive me for the times when I have been too familiar—the times when I have presumed on our relationship and taken my sins too lightly. I want to worship You in spirit and truth. Teach me who You really are. Help me become more intimate with You so that I may become less familiar.

PERSONAL REFLECTIONS

Day Nine

RSVP (Part One)

Protocol of the Palace #4
Worship is the protocol that
protects the King and qualifies the visitor.
Finding Favor With the King, 42

———

SCRIPTURE READING

MATTHEW 22:1–14, IN WHICH JESUS TELLS THE PARABLE OF
A KING'S WEDDING FOR HIS SON. THE INVITED GUESTS
PROVE THEY ARE UNWORTHY BY REFUSING TO COME AND
ARE REPLACED BY THOSE BROUGHT IN FROM THE
"HIGHWAYS." ONE WEDDING GUEST, FOUND WITHOUT
A WEDDING GARMENT, IS EXPELLED INTO
"OUTER DARKNESS."

———

ormal attire required: evening gown; black tie. RSVP.
Have you ever received an invitation like that? If you have, you
know it is going to be a very fancy event. There is a *protocol* to attending.
You've been invited, but to get inside you must be properly dressed.
Otherwise, you'll be stopped at the door (if you get that far).

In Jesus' parable of the wedding, one guest is thrown out because he was not wearing a wedding garment. The implication, of course, is that everyone else was properly dressed for the occasion. This man stood out because he was clearly out of place.

The proper "attire" for admittance to the presence of the King is *worship.* True worship is possible only for those who are in *relationship* with the King. A king relates to the subjects and citizens of his realm differently than he does to visitors from outside. Foreigners may respect and acknowledge a king's power and position as a head of state, but they do not relate to him the same way as those who live daily under his authority. Worship, then, is predicated on relationship. And relationship provides access.

Worship is the protocol that protects the King. How do you protect the King of Kings, who is God and thus impervious to harm? Certainly it does not mean providing physical security as with an earthly king. There are ways, however, for us to "protect" our King.

First, we can protect His *reputation.* We do this by being true to His Word as His ambassadors. We are ambassadors for Christ.[1] As His ambassadors we are charged to speak His Word openly, honestly, and accurately, "rightly dividing the word of truth."[2] Just as with any ambassador of any earthly realm, we represent our King and our word should be His Word. If we say we represent the King and then speak contrary to His Word, we impugn His reputation.

Second, we can protect His *name.* This we do by living according to His standards rather than the standards of the world. It means living honestly and with the highest standard of character and moral and ethical integrity. As children of God we carry the family name. If we live contrary to the standards of our Father and His house, we bring dishonor to His name.

Third, we can protect His *glory.* We do this by being careful to give Him praise at all times. We do it by publicly and privately—at every opportunity—acknowledging Him in all our ways, trusting Him to

---

[1] 2 Corinthians 5:20.
[2] 2 Timothy 2:15.

direct our paths.[3] God has said that He will not give His glory to another.[4] Whenever we take pride in our own gifts or take for ourselves credit that is due Him, we steal His glory.

As children of the King we must be careful how we speak and how we act. The reputation, name, and glory of our Father the King are at stake—in the eyes of men.

===

PRAYER

My God and King, thank You for my relationship in Christ that gives me access to You. With the help of Your Spirit I will protect Your reputation by being true to Your Word. I will protect Your name by living according to Your standards as a faithful son or daughter. I will protect Your glory by acknowledging You in all my ways.

PERSONAL REFLECTIONS

---

[3]Proverbs 3:5–6.
[4]Isaiah 42:8.

Day Ten

RSVP (PART TWO)

Protocol of the Palace #4
Worship is the protocol that
protects the King and qualifies the visitor.
Finding Favor With the King, 42

SCRIPTURE READING

MATTHEW 22:1–14, IN WHICH JESUS TELLS THE PARABLE OF
A KING'S WEDDING FOR HIS SON. THE INVITED GUESTS
PROVE THEY ARE UNWORTHY BY REFUSING TO COME AND
ARE REPLACED BY THOSE BROUGHT IN FROM THE
"HIGHWAYS." ONE WEDDING GUEST, FOUND WITHOUT
A WEDDING GARMENT, IS EXPELLED INTO
"OUTER DARKNESS."

D*o you have an appointment? Please have a seat. Mr.* _____
will be with you shortly.

Protocols are a part of life. We face them every day in one form or another. Whether at security checkpoints, reception areas, switchboards, or the like, standards and procedures are in operation in many places to screen callers, clients, or visitors. This is not only for protection. It is also to help ensure that people with legitimate business get where they need to go and that others are either redirected or turned away.

Just as worship is the protocol that protects the King, it is also the protocol that qualifies the visitor. Remember that worship is predicated on relationship. In Jesus' parable of the wedding, the king spots a guest who has no wedding garment. The wedding garment was a sign of relationship. It was proof that the guest had been invited and had the right to be there. Somehow an interloper had gotten inside. A "wedding crasher" had invaded the party. When he was unable to answer the king's challenge, he was evicted.

Relationship gives us the right of access to the King. Worship is the garment that gets us through the door.

Part of the protocol for qualifying visitors is the protocol of waiting. As I wrote in *Finding Favor With the King* (42), *waiting is worship.* Many of us don't handle waiting very well. This is especially true when we have been praying for something for a while and God seems to be silent. Our fast-paced, microwave-speed, instant-everything society has conditioned us to expect immediate gratification of any desire. Sometimes God lets us wait so that we can learn patience. At other times He delays His answer because He is preparing to give us something better.

Waiting on the Lord rearranges our priorities and reorients our perspective to those of the King. It also gauges how hungry we are for Him. Many would-be visitors to the King's presence disqualify themselves by being unwilling to wait. If their request for an audience is not answered promptly, they leave. They're either too busy or not hungry enough to hang around. And so they miss their opportunity. When their turn finally comes, they are already gone.

Don't let impatience cause you to forfeit your opportunity to see the King. Content yourself with waiting on Him. If you wait long enough your patience will be well rewarded. You will be drawn into an intimacy with the King that is experienced by very few. "Wait on the Lord; be of good courage, and He shall strengthen your heart; wait, I say, on the Lord!"[1]

---

[1]Psalm 27:14.

═══

PRAYER

Lord, thank You for the garment of righteousness You have given me in Christ that gives me the right to come into Your presence. I know that I sometimes get impatient when You don't answer my prayer right away. Forgive me. Grant me patience that I may learn to wait on You and gain entrance to the inner chamber of deeper intimacy with You.

PERSONAL REFLECTIONS

Day Eleven

DIVINE GPS

There is a road map to God's presence . . .
and love stamps your visa.
Finding Favor With the King, 43

═══

SCRIPTURE READING

MATTHEW 11:28–30, IN WHICH JESUS INVITES ALL WHO
LABOR AND ARE HEAVY LADEN TO COME TO HIM AND REST
AND TO TAKE UP HIS YOKE, WHICH IS EASY, AND HIS
BURDEN, WHICH IS LIGHT.

═══

W*here am I? How do I get where I want to go?*
Have you ever gotten lost trying to get to a particular destination in an unfamiliar part of town? Or trying to find a new address in the dark? Or getting turned around and missing an exit during a road trip?

Navigation in the physical world has always been a challenge for man. Over the centuries our skills in this area have grown more and more sophisticated. Today they are nothing short of phenomenal.

One of the most remarkable devices to appear in the technological explosion of the last thirty years is the GPS (Global Positioning System).

With the help of an array of geo-synchronous satellites, this compact device (some even hand-sized) can pinpoint our location by latitude, longitude, and elevation anywhere in the world with an accuracy error of no more than a few feet. Our "global village" has never seemed smaller or more accessible.

And yet despite our incredible capabilities in navigation in the natural world, mankind as a whole still stumbles around in the darkness trying to navigate in the spiritual realm. *How do I find God?* That is the universal question.

God Himself has made the way clear. The *Bible* is the *road map*. It points us in the right direction—to Jesus. The *cross* is the *tollgate*, where the love of God stamps our entry visa. Jesus has already paid the toll—with His blood. *Faith* is the *access ramp* that places us on the highway of eternal life. *Worship* is the *rest area* where we can wait and rest in God's presence and renew our strength for the continuing journey.

The human race as a whole runs itself ragged trying to find God. People pray elaborate prayers, chant mantras, and perform sacrifices and all sorts of intricate and precise rituals—all in an effort to win the favor of the god of their own making. Meanwhile, the one true God has made the way to Him clear.

In Matthew 11:28–30 Jesus invites all who "labor and are heavy laden" to come to Him, take up His yoke, and receive rest for their souls. Jesus' yoke is easy because it is the yoke of grace, not works-based salvation. His burden is light because it is the burden of joyful discipleship and obedience, not guilt and fear.

How do you navigate in the darkness? Dispel the darkness with the Light of the World! Jesus said, "I am the light of the world. He who follows Me shall not walk in darkness, but have the light of life."[1] He is the Light that fills our lives. This is the light that all who stumble in the darkness need to see shining in us.

How do you get into God's presence? Using His "Divine GPS," you discover that as a Christian you are already there! You're right where you ought to be: *wrapped in the arms of your loving Father!*

---

[1]John 8:12.

PRAYER

Father, thank You for Your love and grace that give me unlimited access to Your presence. Thank You for sending Jesus to dispel my darkness and bring me into Your light. Let Your light so shine in me that others can see the way to You.

PERSONAL REFLECTIONS

Day Twelve

NO STRINGS ATTACHED

Praise takes you into His [God's] courts.
Finding Favor With the King, 46

≡

SCRIPTURE READING

PSALM 100, WHICH CALLS ON US TO SHOUT JOYFULLY TO
THE LORD, SING IN HIS PRESENCE, AND ENTER HIS GATES
WITH THANKSGIVING AND HIS COURTS WITH PRAISE.

≡

When was the last time you thanked God for something He gave you or did for you? This morning? Yesterday? Last week? Last month? Giving thanks to God daily is always appropriate because God is always giving. An unthankful heart is a poison to your spirit. Over time it will make you bitter, cynical, and broken. It may even make you physically sick. Thankfulness, on the other hand, will fill you with joy and cause your spirit and body to prosper. A thankful heart is a cheerful heart. The Bible says, "A cheerful heart is good medicine, but a crushed spirit dries up the bones."[1] So take a look around. See

---

[1] Proverbs 17:22 NIV.

what God has done. *If you can't find something in your life to thank God for, you're not looking hard enough!*

Thanksgiving is a form of worship. When you thank God, you acknowledge Him as your Source and Provider of all things. You also express your gratitude for what He has done. Yet thanksgiving, as wonderful and appropriate as it is, is not the highest level of worship. That place belongs to praise. As Psalm 100 says, thanksgiving gets you through the gate, but praise carries you all the way into the King's inner court.

What's the difference? Thanksgiving acknowledges God for what He has done. Praise acknowledges God for *who He is.* So many times our worship is diluted with worldly desires and selfish motives. We worship because we want something from God. God is so gracious, however, that He often honors and blesses us anyway, even when our motivation is not what it should be.

Praise is worship with no strings attached. We come into the King's court with no agenda. Our only motive is to be with Him and enjoy His presence.

When was the last time you truly praised God? How long has it been since you simply acknowledged Him for who He is, with no other agenda? Praise will reorient your thinking. It will give you a whole new perspective. When you are in the King's court, you will see things the way He does.

We all have times when we don't feel like praying, times when it's hard to feel thankful. Those are the times when it is most important of all to praise God. *You can literally praise your way into a thankful and joyful heart.* Try it!

Do you want to draw God near? Then praise Him. No agenda. No strings attached. No ulterior motive. Just praise Him. David the psalmist wrote, "But You are holy, enthroned in the praises of Israel."[2] God always turns His ear to undiluted words of love from His children. Let your praise go up and He will draw you into His inner court!

---

[2]Psalm 22:3.

PRAYER

Father, You are awesome and beautiful beyond description. My God, my Father, my Creator, my Sustainer, my Provider, my Healer, my Redeemer, and my Friend, I love You. You are worthy of all praise and glory and honor and power and wisdom and riches and strength! Your name is above all other names. Your mercy is so great and Your love is so deep. I exalt You!

PERSONAL REFLECTIONS

Day Thirteen

HOW FAR WILL YOU GO?

Protocol of the Palace #9
The deeper you go into the palace,
the fewer the people, but the greater the provision.
Finding Favor With the King, 49

═══

SCRIPTURE READING

LUKE 14:25–33, IN WHICH JESUS LAYS OUT CLEARLY
THE TRUE COST OF DISCIPLESHIP.

═══

Are you a leader or a follower? Do you like blazing new trails? Or are you more comfortable on a well-defined path? Do you regard difficulties as *challenges* or as *setbacks*? Are you the kind of person who will keep pressing in to get what you're after? How far will you go to realize your dreams?

A disciple is one whose dream is to be like Jesus.

Don't confuse being a *Christian* with being a *disciple*. Every believer is a Christian but not every believer is a disciple. Disciples are believers who are committed to going deeper and deeper with the Lord—as deep as they can go. Most believers are content just to be saved. They're just happy to have their ticket to heaven. The demands of the deeper life in Christ don't really attract them.

And with good reason: those demands are high. In Luke 14:25–33 Jesus sets out the demands of discipleship in such terms as bearing a cross, counting the cost, and forsaking all. *Not for the faint of heart!*

The deeper things of the Spirit are reserved for those who are willing and determined to press in and claim them—*to plunge headlong into the wellspring of the very heart of God!*

Paul was this kind of person. He was a trailblazer: "I have made it my aim to preach the gospel, not where Christ was named, lest I should build on another man's foundation."[1] And he was willing to pay any price to touch the heart of Christ: "I . . . count all things loss for the excellence of the knowledge of Christ Jesus my Lord . . . and count them as rubbish, that I may gain Christ . . . that I may know Him and the power of His resurrection, and the fellowship of His sufferings, being conformed to His death."[2] He understood that this would require single-minded determination: "One thing I do, forgetting those things which are behind and reaching forward to those things which are ahead, I press toward the goal for the prize of the upward call of God in Christ Jesus."[3]

You don't have to be a trailblazer to be a disciple. You don't have to be a natural leader. *All you need is an abandoned love for Jesus and a heart that yearns to be like Him.* It's what Jesus calls hungering and thirsting for righteousness—and He promises satisfaction.[4]

The deeper you go into the palace, the fewer the people. Why? Because few people are willing to pay the price of moving deeper. The demands of learning the protocols are too high. What about you? Are you willing? Let me challenge you to go for it. As I wrote in *Finding Favor With the King* (49): "Go where few dare—into the lap of the King." The cost is high, but the reward is worth it. How far will you go?

---

[1]Romans 15:20.
[2]Philippians 3:8–10.
[3]Philippians 3:13b–14.
[4]Matthew 5:6.

===

PRAYER

Lord, I love You. I want to be like You. I want to plunge headlong into Your love and know Your heart. Give me the wisdom to count the cost and the courage to take up my cross. Forsaking all, I will follow You.

PERSONAL REFLECTIONS

Day Fourteen

JUST ASK!

Position and petition often shout their demands,
but passion need only whisper!
Finding Favor With the King, 50

≡

SCRIPTURE READING

MATTHEW 7:7–11, IN WHICH JESUS TELLS US SIMPLY
TO ASK, SEEK, AND KNOCK . . . AND IT WILL BE DONE.
OUR HEAVENLY FATHER WILL GIVE GOOD THINGS
TO ALL WHO ASK.

≡

A*ccess is everything.*
Have you ever noticed how people are always trying to get the ear of the important and the powerful? How they jockey for position in hopes of gaining the advantage over a rival?

Worldly wisdom says that the way to get ahead in life is by outworking, outwitting, or out-shouting the other guy. Grab the attention of the power brokers. Climb in bed with the movers and shakers of the world. Get them on your side, and you've got it made.

That may be the way much of the world operates. But it is not the way things operate in the palace of the King. The way to get the King's ear is not by shouting demands from a position of "legal" access. His ear is tuned instead for the whispered request of a passionate lover. *Passion trumps position.*

A religious mindset believes that God must be coaxed through persuasion or force of argument. Those who *know* the King know better. Someone said that "prayer is not overcoming God's reluctance but laying hold of His willingness." Relationship is the key. Relationship trumps religion.

Relationship gives a level of access that no legal claim could ever hope to match. An old Scottish proverb says, "A pennyweight o' love is worth a pound o' law."[1] Those who are comfortable in their love relationship with the King know that they don't have to plead or beg or shout louder than someone else. All they have to do is *ask.*

Consider Jesus' words in Matthew 7:7: "Ask, and it will be given to you; seek, and you will find; knock, and it will be opened to you." What could be simpler? There is nothing here about shouting. Nothing about a legal claim or demand. Nothing about an attention-getting demonstration. Just ask, seek, and knock. Jesus goes on in verse 11 to say that the Father willingly gives "good things to those who ask Him."

The King *loves* to give gifts to His children. Jesus said, "Do not fear, little flock, for it is your Father's good pleasure to give you the kingdom."[2] He also gave us this promise: "And whatever things you ask in prayer, believing, you will receive."[3]

There is more power in the whispered word of a passionate lover than in the loudest legal claim. Nothing stirs the heart of the King like the quiet voice of one of His own speaking in love. "Prayer is the soul's sincere desire, unuttered or expressed, the motion of a hidden fire that trembles in the breast. Prayer is the burden of a sigh, the falling of a tear, the upward glancing of an eye, when none but God is near."[4]

Do you want to draw the ear of the King? Relationship gives you

---

[1]Quoted in Frank S. Mead, ed., *12,000 Religious Quotations* (Grand Rapids: Baker Book House, 1965, reprinted 1989, sixth printing 2000), 285.
[2]Luke 12:32.
[3]Matthew 21:22.
[4]James Montgomery, "Prayer Is the Soul's Sincere Desire," hymn in the public domain.

access, and access is everything. His heart is already inclined toward you. So don't beg or plead. Don't shout or demand. Simply speak from a heart of passionate love, and He will answer. *Just ask!*

===

PRAYER

Father, I'm so amazed that You love me so much that all I have to do is ask and You will answer! Teach me to know Your heart and mind so that my requests will always be in line with Your will.

PERSONAL REFLECTIONS

Day Fifteen

THE PROTOCOL OF HUMILITY

How do you move from "powerless" to "powerful"?
Learn the protocol of the palace!
Finding Favor With the King, 53

===

SCRIPTURE READING

PHILIPPIANS 2:5–11, IN WHICH PAUL DESCRIBES HOW JESUS
HUMBLED HIMSELF, BECAME OBEDIENT TO THE POINT OF
DEATH, AND THEN WAS HIGHLY EXALTED AND GIVEN THE
NAME THAT IS ABOVE EVERY NAME.

===

If you want to succeed, you've got to play by the rules.
Only those who master protocol will wield power and influence. And the secret to mastering protocol is learning to play by the rules. Here's one of the rules: *Everything in the palace is set up to advance and fulfill the will of the King!* The King's palace is no place for personal agendas. Power in the palace resides with those who are totally committed to doing the King's will and attending to the welfare of His kingdom.

Sometimes the King changes the protocol. Or at least streamlines the process. As I wrote in *Finding Favor With the King* (53), "Jesus Christ, our high priest, has torn the veil that separates us from God's presence. Now we can enter His presence through a new and living way (or 'protocol')—through the blood of Jesus and through His finished work." Many liturgical churches follow the tradition of painting the doors to their sanctuaries red. Red symbolizes the blood of Christ through which all must pass to enter the family of God and gain access to His presence.

The path from powerless to powerful leads through the sin-cleansing blood of Jesus. Our next step is to understand where our power comes from. We have no power of our own. Just like an electrical appliance has power only when it is plugged into an outlet, we have power only when we are connected to Christ. Jesus said, "I am the vine, you are the branches. He who abides in Me, and I in him, bears much fruit; for without Me you can do nothing."[1] Acts 1:8 says that we receive power from the Holy Spirit. This power is not our own. Nor do we receive it for our benefit or blessing alone. The Lord gives us power so that we can be His witnesses and bless others in His name.

The posture of power in the King's palace is *humility.* Jesus demonstrated this in His own life. Paul said that Jesus "made Himself of no reputation. . . . He humbled Himself and became obedient to the point of death."[2] As a result, God "has highly exalted Him and given Him the name which is above every name."[3] The day will come when every knee will bow and every tongue will confess that Jesus Christ is Lord.

The *truly* powerful do not use their power to show off or to impress people. Jesus never performed a miracle on demand. He never used His power and influence for His own ends but only to accomplish the will of His Father.

Esther found herself in a place of great power and influence. She was queen to the most powerful ruler in the world. Yet she did not use her power to advance her own wealth and prestige. Instead, she put her life on the line and used her influence to save her people.

---

[1]John 15:5.
[2]Philippians 2:7–8.
[3]Philippians 2:9.

Influence in the King's palace lies with those who will humble themselves. Jesus said that greatness in the kingdom of God is measured by *serving*, not by being served. Do you want to have power and influence with the King? Follow the path of selfless service, just as Jesus did. *Practice the protocol of humility.*

═══

PRAYER

Father, thank You for the blood of Jesus that cleanses me of sin and gives me open access to Your presence. Forgive me for pursuing my own agenda while pretending to pursue Yours. Give me a servant's heart. Help me practice the protocol of humility. Let me be a vessel through whom Your power flows for Your purposes and Yours alone.

PERSONAL REFLECTIONS

Day Sixteen

LOVE: THE HEART OF WORSHIP

There are some who love Him simply because He is.
Finding Favor With the King, 56

≡

SCRIPTURE READING

MARK 12:28–34, IN WHICH JESUS EXPLAINS THAT THE
GREATEST COMMANDMENT OF ALL IS TO LOVE GOD WITH
ALL OUR HEART, SOUL, MIND, AND STRENGTH.

≡

Nothing warms the hearts of parents more than to receive the pure, undiluted love of their children. Every time any of my daughters flashed her "I love you, Daddy" smile at me, my heart simply melted. Those were the times I would have tried to give them the moon if they had asked for it! There's something about the innocent, unaffected love of a child that makes a parent willing to do almost anything for her.

God is much the same way. He loves to give good things to His children. Giving is His nature, and He gives lavishly. But God especially loves it when we come to Him and spend time with Him not because we want something, but simply because we love Him and want to be with Him.

In the eyes of the world love usually comes with conditions: "I'll love you *if . . .*" or "I'll love you *when . . .*" or "I love you *because . . .*" Love with no strings attached and no ulterior motive is a rare commodity in the world. I'm talking about *unconditional* love, the kind of love that says, "I love you . . . *period.*" This is the kind of love that God shows toward us. It is also the kind of love He is looking for from us in return.

The Westminster Catechism, one of the classic historical confessions of the church, says, "The chief end of man is to glorify God and enjoy Him forever." How do we glorify God? By doing what He created us to do. *And He created us to love Him.*

One day a Jewish scribe asked Jesus to identify the most important commandment in the law. "Jesus answered him, 'The first of all the commandments is: "Hear, O Israel, the Lord our God, the Lord is one. And you shall love the Lord your God with all your heart, with all your soul, with all your mind, and with all your strength." This is the first commandment.'"[1] The verses that follow state that loving God is more important than burnt offerings and sacrifices. In other words, loving God is more important than all the various things we "do" that we sometimes call "church." *Loving God is the heart of worship.*

Few Christians ever reach the point of worshiping God at that level. For most of us, our love for God extends as far as our gratitude for what He has done for us. The real challenge is to keep pressing upward into the rarefied atmosphere of those who love God simply for who He is, totally apart from anything He has done. Loving and worshiping God at the level of thanksgiving for blessings and favor is okay. But there is a deeper level—the level of praise and adoration—available for those who dare to press into it. This is the level where the deepest intimacy and fellowship with God occurs. This is the level of *true friendship with God.*

Loving God with all your heart, soul, mind, and strength means

---

[1]Mark 12:29–30.

loving Him with everything you are, every moment of the day. It means abandoning yourself to a radical, reckless, passionate love for Him, a love in which your greatest happiness comes in simply being in His presence.

Are you up to the challenge? Take the plunge. Come back to the heart of worship. With everything you are, love God simply for who He is!

=====

PRAYER

Father, I accept the challenge. I am eternally grateful to You for all that You have done for me. But I want to move beyond that level. I want to enter the heart of worship and love You for who You are—with all that I am!

PERSONAL REFLECTIONS

Day Seventeen

GOD'S OPEN HOUSE

The protocol of worship will usher an uninvited interloper into a "throne zone" experience.
Finding Favor With the King, 57

═══

SCRIPTURE READING

LUKE 18:10–14, WHICH IS JESUS' PARABLE OF THE PHARISEE AND THE TAX COLLECTOR PRAYING IN THE TEMPLE. THE PHARISEE LEAVES UNCHANGED, BUT THE TAX COLLECTOR GOES HOME "JUSTIFIED" BECAUSE HE APPROACHED GOD IN HUMBLE REPENTANCE.

═══

G*od hates dividing lines.*
Isn't it great that God doesn't run His kingdom the way many of us run our churches? Otherwise, very few of us would get in! One of the great sins of the church through the ages is the placing of all sorts of man-made restrictions on who can come in—restrictions that God never sanctioned or commanded. Churches have divided over racial lines, ethnic lines, socioeconomic lines, educational lines, and just about any other line you could name.

God hates dividing lines, especially when they keep people away from Him. That's why when Jesus died the veil in the temple was torn from top to bottom. Open access of man to God was now available. That's why when true revival breaks out, man-made walls come down so that anyone who wishes may come in and drink from the fountain of life.

In 1901, William Seymour, a preacher hungry for the things of the Spirit, wanted to learn about the new Pentecostal outpourings that were taking place at Charles Parham's Bible school. Being black, Seymour was not allowed inside the building. So he sat on the steps outside and listened through the window. And God touched him. Five years later William Seymour was the catalyst God used to spark the Azusa Street revival. William Seymour: uninvited by man but welcomed by God!

The self-righteous Pharisee in Jesus' parable undoubtedly believed that the tax collector had no business even being in the temple. After all, the house of God was no place for the likes of him! On the contrary: *God wants His house open to all who desire to enter!* God has said, "For My house shall be called a house of prayer for all nations."[1] To the Pharisee, the tax collector was an uninvited interloper. To God, he was a beloved and welcome son, a prodigal returning home.

Jesus said that the Pharisee went home that day unchanged. He was so full of himself that there was no room for God. The Pharisee, despite his vast knowledge of the Law, had never learned the protocol of worship. Therefore, he never made it into the presence of God.

The tax collector, on the other hand, followed the proper protocol of worship. He entered in a spirit of humility and repentance: "God, be merciful to me a sinner!"[2] This gained him access to the King. Jesus said he went home "justified." The tax collector received a "throne-zone" experience that changed him forever.

What about you? No matter who you are, the King welcomes you. No matter where you've been or what you've done, the King says, "Come to Me." Don't let the false rules or misguided perceptions of men keep you from your "throne-zone" experience with the King. Practice the

[1]Isaiah 56:7b.
[2]Luke 18:13b.

protocols of humility and worship. You will discover that the door to the King's throne room is always open!

═══

PRAYER

Lord, thank You for welcoming me into Your house. Thank You for forgiving my sins and changing my life. Forgive me for judging or ranking others by human standards. With Your Spirit's help I will welcome in Your name everyone I meet. I will help them learn the protocols for gaining access to Your throne.

PERSONAL REFLECTIONS

Day Eighteen

LET GOD TURN YOU AROUND

He can alter your destiny and change your reputation.
Finding Favor With the King, 59

═══

SCRIPTURE READING

ACTS 9:1–20, WHERE SAUL OF TARSUS MEETS CHRIST ON
THE ROAD TO DAMASCUS, WHICH ALTERS HIS DESTINY AND
CHANGES HIS REPUTATION. THIS ENEMY OF THE CHURCH
IS TRANSFORMED INTO A BOLD AND PASSIONATE
DISCIPLE OF CHRIST.

═══

Y*our destiny is not fixed.*
Do you sometimes feel that the mistakes of your past are holding you back? Are you afraid that through poor choices you have squandered all your opportunities to live the life you once dreamed of? Is your life full of guilt and regret? Do you sometimes wish you could turn the clock back and start over?

Unfortunately, you can't relive your past. But your past does not have to determine your future. Turn your future over to God, and He can turn it around. He can alter your destiny and change your reputation.

Just consider Jacob, the "deceiver," who cheated his brother Esau out of his birthright. Later, however, Jacob wrestled with God. God changed his name to Israel, meaning "prince of God," and made him the father of the nation that bore his name.

Then there's Moses, a murderer and fugitive in the desert, whose destiny was altered at a burning bush. His encounter with God changed him into a deliverer who freed a nation from slavery.

Zacchaeus, a despised tax collector, hosted Jesus as a houseguest one day. That encounter so transformed him that it prompted Jesus to say, "Today salvation has come to this house."[1]

God is in the destiny-altering and reputation-changing business. Just look at Saul. On his way to Damascus to arrest followers of Christ, he met the Lord on the road. Blinded temporarily by the encounter, Saul rested at the home of a man named Judas. In the meantime, God instructed Ananias to go to Saul and restore his sight, saying, "Go, for he is a chosen vessel of Mine to bear My name before Gentiles, kings, and the children of Israel."[2] Saul thought his destiny was to rid the land of Jesus-followers, but God altered his destiny. As Paul he became one of the most potent forces in spreading the gospel of Christ throughout the Roman Empire in the first century.

God changed Paul's reputation too. When he first tried to mingle with other believers, they didn't trust him. They thought he was trying to trick them. Before long, however, when they saw how he was boldly preaching the faith he once tried to destroy, they glorified God because of him.[3]

What God did for Paul and all these others He can do for you. Do you feel like you have really messed up your life? God can straighten things out and set you on the right road. There is no sin so great that God's grace is not greater still, no hole so deep that God's love cannot reach you and pull you out. Remember that one day of favor can be worth more than a lifetime of labor. At the same time, *one day of favor*

---

[1]Luke 19:9.
[2]Acts 9:15.
[3]Galatians 1:23–24.

can change a lifetime of mistakes, bad choices, and missed opportunities.

Don't let the shame or discouragement of your past rob you of your future. Turn to the One who can alter your destiny and change your reputation. *Let God turn you around!*

≡

PRAYER

Father, I know I have made a lot of bad choices. I've messed up my life in many ways. But now I'm turning it over to You. Take control of my life and my destiny. Turn me around and set me on the road to the destiny You have always had for me. Let my life be a testimony to Your transforming power.

PERSONAL REFLECTIONS

Day Nineteen

ARE YOU ONE OF GOD'S FAVORITES?

God is no respecter of persons, but He does *play favorites.*
Finding Favor With the King, 60

═══

SCRIPTURE READING

PSALM 89:1–4, 19–37, IN WHICH THE LORD DECLARES THE
COVENANT AND PROMISE HE HAS MADE TO DAVID, TO
ESTABLISH HIS KINGDOM FOREVER.

═══

A *re you one of God's favorites?*
God is no respecter of persons.[1] His invitation to intimacy is open to anyone and everyone. Not everyone, however, will accept the invitation. Many people dream of intimacy with the King. For most of them it will remain only a dream. In the final analysis they are unwilling to learn the protocol of worship that will make their dream come true. Or they feel unworthy and assume that such intimacy is beyond their reach.

Worthiness has nothing to do with it. None of us is *worthy* to enter

---

[1]Acts 10:34.

the presence of the King. The blood of Jesus makes us worthy. Because of Jesus' finished work on the cross, we can enter into intimacy with our heavenly Father. All we have to do is learn the protocol of the palace.

As Creator, God loves all people equally. He does, however, have a special place in His heart for those who become His spiritual children through faith in Christ. But even among believers there are those who press in further to become His special favorites. This is not because God loves them more than He loves others. It is because they have gone to the trouble to learn what He favors.

God's favorites are those who have determined to make Him their absolute top priority. They are the ones who have freely chosen to love Him with all their heart, soul, mind, and strength. With this choice they have forsaken all else in order to have Him. They have abandoned themselves to God and to the knowing of His heart and mind. These are the ones for whom God will move heaven and earth.

Are you one of them? You can be!

David was one of them. Psalm 89 describes God's covenant with David. God promised David that He would establish his seed forever and build up his throne to all generations.[2] He promised to give David success and victory over his enemies. God promised to keep David's descendants on the throne even if not all of them followed Him faithfully! What was it about David that gained him such favor with God?

The Bible says that David was a man after God's own heart.[3] In other words, David was a God-chaser. David's greatest desire was to know God and do His will. He walked in daily fellowship with God. David loved God with a passion and worshiped Him with radical and reckless abandon. This made David one of God's "favorites."

God is no respecter of persons, but He *does* play favorites. And *you* can be one of His favorites. Learn the protocol of worship. Love God with all your heart, soul, mind, and strength. Let go of anything in your life that could challenge God for first place or hinder your pursuit of

---

[2]Psalm 89:3–4.
[3]1 Samuel 13:14; Acts 13:22.

Him. Press in and accept God's invitation to intimacy. *Become one of God's favorites!*

———

PRAYER

Father, I want to be one of Your favorites. You have invited me to the place of intimacy with You. Forsaking all else as first in my life, I choose You as my supreme love. As I seek to worship You with passionate abandon, draw me into Your intimate embrace.

PERSONAL REFLECTIONS

Day Twenty

LET YOUR LIGHT SHINE

*Worship is how you handle yourself
in the presence of the King.*
Finding Favor With the King, 61

SCRIPTURE READING

MATTHEW 5:1–16, IN WHICH JESUS DESCRIBES THE
CHARACTER AND BEHAVIOR OF CHILDREN OF THE KING,
CHARACTER AND BEHAVIOR THAT REFLECT A LIFESTYLE
OF WORSHIP.

W*orship is a lifestyle.*
Once you have entered the King's inner chamber and enjoyed the intimacy of His presence you will never be the same again. Everything looks different from the King's perspective. The panorama of that viewpoint will alter forever the way you look at the world and at life itself. It will even change the way you behave. Some have called this experience being "ruined for the ordinary."

Esther prepared for an entire year for her one night with the king. She had no guarantee that she would ever see him again after that one encounter. Yet no matter the outcome, she would never return to her old way of life. Never again would she be just a peasant girl from a conquered nation. From that day forward she walked, talked, and carried herself like the queen she was groomed to be—like the queen she *became*. Esther prepared carefully and diligently for one night with the king, but her queenly demeanor became a *lifestyle*.

For the King's favorites, worship is not something that happens just in church on Sunday. Neither is it confined to the quiet times we spend alone in God's presence. Once we learn the protocol of the palace—the protocol of intimate worship—that protocol becomes (or should become) our way of life. Everywhere we go we will carry ourselves like the King's intimates that we are. This does not mean we will act arrogantly or boast of our position. It does mean that *we will live in such a way as to reflect the heart and character of the King*. We will act like His children no matter where we are or what our circumstances may be.

Because the King abides in us through His Holy Spirit, we carry His presence with us wherever we go. Therefore, every moment of every day becomes an opportunity and a reason for worship. Worship is how we handle ourselves in the presence of the King. *Worship is not what we do; it is who we are!* We are worshipers by nature. As the King's intimates and favorites, our entire lives should be a continuing act of worship!

In Matthew 5 Jesus described the character of the King's children. He said that they are poor in spirit, mournful (over the sin of the world), meek (gentle), hungry and thirsty for righteousness, merciful, pure in heart, and peacemakers. He also said they are persecuted for the sake of righteousness. In short, they exhibit the character of their father, the King. Summing it all up, Jesus said, "Let your light so shine before men, that they may see your good works and glorify your Father in heaven."[1] That's what a lifestyle of worship is all about.

As children of the King, everything we do or say reflects on His name and character, either for good or bad. Ask yourself: *Is my daily life a continuing act of worship? Do my words and behavior draw people to the King or drive them away?*

---

[1] Matthew 5:16.

Let your life become an ongoing offering of worship to your King. Let His character and heart that fill you during those intimate encounters with Him spill over onto the lives of others. Let your light shine!

=====

PRAYER

Father, sometimes I forget that worship is not something I do but who I am. Forgive me for all the times when my words or actions have reflected poorly on You. Draw me into You in such a way that my whole life becomes a continual offering of worship to You. "Let the words of my mouth and the meditation of my heart be acceptable in Your sight, O Lord, my strength and my Redeemer." [2]

PERSONAL REFLECTIONS

---

[2]Psalm 19:14.

Day Twenty-One

THE INSIDE TRACK

Protocol of the Palace #5
Influence flows from intimacy,
and access comes from relationship.
Finding Favor With the King, 65

───

SCRIPTURE READING

JOHN 15:11–17, WHERE JESUS COMMANDS HIS DISCIPLES TO
LOVE ONE ANOTHER. HE CALLS THEM HIS FRIENDS, BY
WHICH RELATIONSHIP THEY CAN ASK WHATEVER THEY
WISH AND IT WILL BE GIVEN TO THEM.

───

Relationship will give you access that petitioners only dream of.
John F. Kennedy was one of the few American presidents to have very young children in the White House. One well-known photograph shows President Kennedy in the Oval Office meeting with several of his advisers. Everything looks quite businesslike and professional—except for the face of little "John-John" peering out from underneath his daddy's desk. Serious matters of state were discussed on a daily basis. High levels of security and tight protocols protected the president from everyday intrusions. Yet little John Jr. always had ready access to his

father, the most powerful man in the free world.

Many dream of access to the rich and powerful but few ever achieve it. Those who do, usually spend many years preparing and positioning themselves for it. The Bible says that a man's gift makes room for him and brings him before great men[1] and also that he who excels in his work will stand before kings and rulers.[2] But relationship trumps both preparation and gifts. Relationship affords intimate access that even the most gifted and talented "outsiders" can only envy.

In John 15:12, Jesus commands his disciples to love one another, a love based on their *relationship* with Him. Then He says: "No longer do I call you servants, for a servant does not know what his master is doing; but I have called you friends, for all things that I heard from My Father I have made known to you."[3] "Friend" is a level of relationship that a servant can never know. Servants, because of their duties, have a certain level of access but never attain the intimacy enjoyed by a friend. Our friendship with Jesus gives us access to Him and a level of intimacy unknown to those who have no relationship with Him.

Jesus is more than just our friend, however; He is also our Elder Brother. The Bible says that we are heirs of God and joint heirs with Christ. This means we are "kin." Our relationship as "family" gives us access that no one outside the family enjoys. This is why Jesus taught in parables to the crowds but explained his teachings in detail to His disciples. It is also why He promised them that anything they asked of the Father in His name they would receive.[4] Their relationship with Him gave them an "inside track" to His heart and mind.

The same is true for you. As a believer you already have the relationship that will give you intimate access to Jesus. That intimacy gives you great influence in the courts of heaven. Don't stay outside on the fringe of the crowd. Press in to receive the fullness of intimacy that is yours for the asking. Offer up pure and unadorned worship of your King. *Get on the inside track!*

---

[1]Proverbs 18:16.
[2]Proverbs 22:29.
[3]John 15:15.
[4]John 15:16.

PRAYER

Lord, I love You and want to be on the inside track with You. And I know that's where You want me to be. Bring me into the fullness of intimacy that my relationship with You affords.

PERSONAL REFLECTIONS

Day Twenty-Two

THE PARADISE OF HIS PRESENCE

*Intimacy with Christ is more powerful
than petitions legally presented.*
Finding Favor With the King, 66

≡

SCRIPTURE READING

LUKE 23:39–43, IN WHICH ONE OF THE THIEVES CRUCIFIED
WITH JESUS ASKS THE LORD TO REMEMBER HIM WHEN HE
COMES INTO HIS KINGDOM, AND JESUS REPLIES THAT THEY
WILL BE IN PARADISE TOGETHER.

≡

*L*ove trumps legalism.

Our American judicial system is based on the principle that every legitimate claimant is entitled to his day in court. In the courts of heaven, however, we have no such right. Because of our sin, we have no *legal* standing before God. We have no legitimate claim that we can make on His blessings or favor. The only basis we have for standing before God is His *grace*. The only hope we have of being accepted by God is on the basis of Jesus' completed work on the cross. Legal claims will never get us into the King's throne room. Intimacy with Christ

based on a faith relationship with Him *will,* because love trumps legalism.

The thief on the cross understood this intuitively. He knew that he
had no legal leg to stand on. No legal petition in the world would have
gotten him off of that cross and spared his life. Not only was he suffering
the judgment of Rome for his crimes, he also faced the coming judgment of God for his sins.

In such a desperate situation, he did the only thing he could do. He
cut straight to the chase and asked for mercy of the only Person who
could give it to him: the Man hanging on the cross next to him. Can
you imagine the *faith* of this thief asking a *dying man* to remember him
when He came into His kingdom? In a last-minute but genuine act of
faith the thief appealed for grace and mercy—and received them. His
faith overrode all legal considerations and gained him instant intimacy
with the Lord and access to the kingdom of heaven.

Even in the closing hours of his life, this thief recognized Jesus for
who He was and made his humble, repentant request. Humility and
repentance are protocols that lead directly to the King's throne room.
Combined with his faith and love, they gained this thief the immediate ear of the King. His appeal based on love and intimacy achieved
for him what no legal petition could ever have accomplished. He
found forgiveness and the promise of eternal fellowship in the presence of the Lord.

Like the thief on the cross, our access to the Father is based not on
any legal claim but on the intimacy we have with Christ through our
faith relationship with Him. That intimacy is more powerful than any
legal claim. Intimacy will bring us closer to the heart of God than any
amount of claiming our "rights" as children of God. Don't settle for
simply standing on your rights. Move in closer. Draw near to God in
love and He will draw near to you. Like the thief on the cross, you will
discover that you too can be with Him today in the paradise of His
presence!

═══

PRAYER

Father, I have no legal claim on Your love or favor. All I have is Your grace, mercy, and love . . . and they are all I need. Thank You for loving me and accepting me through Christ, my Lord. Draw near to me even as I seek to draw near to You. Let me walk today in the paradise of Your presence!

PERSONAL REFLECTIONS

Day Twenty-Three

YOUR HEART'S DESIRE

When you seek His face, your heavenly Father sees your face
and interrupts the business of heaven to bend down and
inquire about your needs!
Finding Favor With the King, 66–67

SCRIPTURE READING

PSALM 27, WHERE DAVID STATES THAT HIS ONE DESIRE IS
TO DWELL IN THE HOUSE OF THE LORD, BEHOLD THE
BEAUTY OF THE LORD, AND SEEK THE LORD'S FACE.

N*othing attracts God's attention like the face of one of His beloved children.*

God is by nature a face-to-face God. In the garden of Eden Adam and Eve enjoyed daily face-to-face contact with their Creator. After their disobedience, they hid from His face in fear as He walked in the garden in the cool of the day.[1]

Ever since then no human being has seen God's face directly. The Bible says that God "spoke to Moses face to face, as a man speaks to his

---

[1]Genesis 3:8.

friend."[2] But even this face-to-face encounter apparently was not in a physical sense. When Moses asked to see God's glory, God told him: "You cannot see My face; for no man shall see Me, and live."[3] Instead, God placed Moses in the cleft of a rock, covered him with His hand until He had passed by, and then allowed Moses to see His back.

In the same way, we cannot see the face of God directly because the brilliance of His glory would kill us. The closest thing to seeing God face to face was to see Jesus in the flesh. When Philip said, "Lord, show us the Father," Jesus replied, "He who has seen Me has seen the Father."[4] The day will come when all of us who are children of God will see Him face to face. Then we will be like Him because we will see Him as He is.[5]

Until then the Lord invites us and encourages us to seek His face in prayer and in intimate communion. Like the loving Father He is, He delights to see our faces. And when we seek His face in prayer and in worship He hastens to bend His ear to our voice. When we love Him, He dotes on us. Jesus said that the Father is pleased to give us the kingdom.[6] Paul said that God, who willingly gave up His Son for us, will also freely give us all things.[7]

David understood this fatherly giving nature of God. That is why he said, "One thing I have desired of the Lord, that I will seek: that I may dwell in the house of the Lord all the days of my life, to behold the beauty of the Lord, and to inquire in His temple. . . . When You said, 'Seek My face,' my heart said to You, 'Your face, Lord, I will seek.'"[8]

David was a man after God's own heart. In love he sought—and found—the face of God. Follow David's example. Your heavenly Father is always looking, eagerly desiring, to see your face. Seek His face and He will interrupt the business of heaven to listen to you. Delight yourself in Him and He will give you your heart's desire![9]

---

[2]Exodus 33:11.
[3]Exodus 33:20.
[4]John 14:8–9.
[5]1 John 3:2.
[6]Luke 12:32.
[7]Romans 8:32.
[8]Psalm 27:4, 8.
[9]Psalm 37:4.

====

PRAYER

Father, I will seek Your face because I love You and because I know You delight in seeing me. I will delight myself in You so that You will give me the desires of my heart. And let my greatest desire be You!

PERSONAL REFLECTIONS

Day Twenty-Four

TAKE A TIMEOUT!

Relationship is cultured, not automatic.
Finding Favor With the King, 68

≡

SCRIPTURE READING

GENESIS 5:21–24; HEBREWS 11:5–6, WHICH SPEAK OF ENOCH,
WHO "WALKED WITH GOD" FOR 300 YEARS AND "WAS NOT,"
BECAUSE "GOD TOOK HIM," A GREAT EXAMPLE OF
THE REWARD THAT COMES TO THOSE WHO DILIGENTLY
SEEK GOD.

≡

Some things can't be rushed. Building a strong relationship is one of them.

The only way to really get to know someone is by spending time with that person. Lots of time. That is why "long-distance" relationships rarely survive over the long-term. Absence may make the heart grow fonder, but it also makes the memories grow weaker. Sustained separation will cause a once close relationship to fade into a distant memory. A close and intimate relationship can be sustained only by close and intimate contact on a regular basis. This is true of any human relationship.

It is also true of our relationship with God. Have you ever noticed how easy it is to start taking your relationship with God for granted? To allow the urgent demands of the day and the routine pressures of life to push aside your intimate moments with the King? When things are going well it is very easy to let your relationship with God slip into "autopilot." Before long you begin to presume on that relationship. You start thinking, *God is always there if I need Him.* But when a crisis comes and you really *do* need Him, you often find that your communication tools have become rusty through disuse.

Indeed, God *is* always there, but a strong relationship is a two-way street. A strong relationship is cultured over time. It is not automatic. We find this principle illustrated over and over in the Bible. Enoch is a good example. Genesis says that "Enoch walked with God three hundred years . . . and he was not, for God took him."[1] Did you notice that? Enoch walked with God for *three hundred years*! He took the time to cultivate his relationship with God, and God rewarded him by bringing Enoch into His presence permanently. Enoch is one of only two humans who have ever bypassed death. (Elijah is the other one.)

Hebrews 11:5 says that Enoch's testimony was that he "pleased God." The next verse states that without faith it is impossible to please God, but that God is a "rewarder of those who *diligently seek Him.*"[2]

Do you want to be close to God? Then take the time to cultivate your relationship. Diligently seek the Lord. God desires an intimate relationship with you more than you do. But He will not force the issue. He will try to draw you near. His Spirit will nudge you and prompt you. But the choice of how close and intimate with God you become is yours alone. It all depends on how hungry you are and how determined you are to press in. You can't get close to God "on-the-fly." What's your rush? Slow down. Take the time to walk with Him every day. Your patient, faithful investment of time will bring in a rich return of intimacy with the King. *Take a timeout!*

---

[1] Genesis 5:22, 24.
[2] Hebrews 11:6, emphasis added.

≡

PRAYER

Father, forgive me for the times when I've been too busy for You. I want to be close and intimate with You more than anything else in this world. Help me to slow down and take the time to get to know You. By Your grace I will walk with You and seek Your face every day.

PERSONAL REFLECTIONS

Day Twenty-Five

BE ALL THAT YOU CAN BE

The only way to gain access to the things of God's kingdom is through relationship with the King.
Finding Favor With the King, 69

═══

SCRIPTURE READING

JEREMIAH 31:31–34, WHERE GOD ANNOUNCES THE NEW COVENANT THAT HE WILL WRITE ON THE HEARTS OF HIS PEOPLE, IN WHICH ALL OF THEM—FROM THE GREATEST TO THE LEAST—WILL KNOW HIM.

═══

Y *ou cannot access what you do not possess.*
There are many pretenders, spiritual "wannabes" who try to scheme their way into the King's throne room. Rather than learn the protocols of the court, they try to sneak in by hook or by crook. Outwardly, they may appear quite "spiritual." But it is only on the surface. Inside, there is nothing there. They are like the Pharisees that Jesus described as whitewashed tombs: outwardly beautiful and righteous but inwardly full of dead men's bones and hypocrisy.[1]

---

[1] Matthew 23:27–28.

Paul described this kind of person as "having a form of godliness but denying its power."[2] After all, you can't exercise the *power* of the King unless you *know* the King. In Acts 19 the seven sons of Sceva tried to exorcise a demon using secondhand faith, appealing to the demon in the name of "Jesus whom Paul preaches."[3] The demon answered, "Jesus I know, and Paul I know; but who are you?"[4] Then the demon attacked them, wounded them, and chased them away.[5] These men did not really know Jesus. All they wanted to do was enhance their reputation as professional exorcists.

Access to the power and possessions of the King is reserved for those who know the King. The full resources of God's kingdom are available to all who walk with Him in an ongoing love relationship. Jesus told his disciples they would receive power when the Holy Spirit came upon them.[6] The Holy Spirit is God's "down payment," His stamp of ownership of us. The Spirit's presence in our lives proves that we are in relationship with Him and guarantees that all of God's promises to us will be fulfilled.

In Jeremiah chapter 31 God promises a new covenant by which His people will be identified: "But this is the covenant that I will make with the house of Israel . . . I will put My law in their minds, and write it on their hearts; and I will be their God, and they shall be My people. . . . They all shall know Me, from the least of them to the greatest of them."[7] Covenant gives formal expression to an existing relationship and imbues it with legal authority. When we are in covenant with the King we have access to His kingdom, His power, and everything that belongs to Him. We can speak in His name, exercise His authority, and appropriate His power and His gifts in carrying out His will.

As a child of the King you are already in covenant with Him. Your relationship with Him gives you access to all that is His. There is one

---

[2] 2 Timothy 3:5.
[3] Acts 19:13.
[4] Acts 19:15.
[5] Acts 19:16.
[6] Acts 1:8.
[7] Jeremiah 31:33–34.

stipulation, however: Everything you do must be for His glory and not your own. Take advantage of your royal rights. Use the King's resources to help you become all that the King desires for you. *Be all that you can be!*

―――

PRAYER

Father, thank You for the relationship that gives me access to You. Help me to use wisely Your resources to become all that I can be according to Your purpose and plan.

PERSONAL REFLECTIONS

Day Twenty-Six

THE POWER
OF A WHISPER

Whispered words from the place of intimacy can be more
powerful than shouted petitions from the court.
Finding Favor With the King, 71

≡

SCRIPTURE READING

MATTHEW 6:5–13, IN WHICH JESUS COUNSELS US NOT TO
PRAY LOUDLY FOR SHOW ON THE STREET CORNERS OR
WITH THE "VAIN REPETITIONS" OF MANY WORDS, BUT
PRIVATELY TO OUR FATHER IN THE SECRET PLACE, WHO
WILL REWARD US OPENLY. JESUS THEN GIVES US THE
LORD'S PRAYER AS A MODEL.

≡

There is great power in a simple whisper.
Experienced classroom teachers have long known that a whisper is the most effective way to regain the attention of an unruly class. Even the rowdiest of students will become silent and strain their ears to hear the whispered words of their teacher. Why? Whispering has a natural calming effect on the mind and the emotions. When someone whispers

we listen closely because we think that otherwise we may miss hearing something important.

The whisper is powerful also because it is the voice of intimacy. Spouses in an intimate setting do not need to shout or even speak in normal tones. A whisper is quite sufficient for sharing thoughts and feelings intended for no one's ears but their own.

God loves the soft hush of a whispered voice. In fact, it is His preferred method of speaking, particularly to all who share an intimate relationship with Him. That is why it is important for us to develop the discipline of silence as part of our worship. Sometimes God speaks to us in a whisper, and we must be quiet if we are to hear Him. Once, when God spoke to Elijah, His coming was preceded by a strong wind, an earthquake, and a fire, but He was not found in any of these. Afterward, He spoke to Elijah in a "still small voice."[1] In Psalm 46:10 He says, "Be still, and know that I am God." The prophet Habakkuk declares: "The Lord is in His holy temple. Let all the earth keep silence before Him."[2]

God likes to speak to us in soft tones. It stands to reason, then, that He prefers us to speak to Him in the same way. When we are on intimate terms with the Lord, there is no need for us to shout. All we have to do is whisper. This is what Jesus had in mind in Matthew chapter 6 when He taught His disciples about prayer. He told us not to pray loudly on the street corners to be seen by people. Nor are we to use "vain repetitions" of "many words."[3] Neither of these will gain us the Father's ear. But He *will* hear the soft voice of intimacy that we raise to Him from the privacy of that secret place where we commune with Him regularly. Poet Alfred Lord Tennyson wrote, "More things are wrought by prayer than this world dreams of."[4] James said, "The effective, fervent prayer of a righteous man avails much."[5] And most of that effective prayer rises to the Father through the whispered words of His children spoken from the secret place. Whispered words of intimacy always carry

---

[1] 1 Kings 19:11–12.
[2] Habakkuk 2:20.
[3] Matthew 6:5–7.
[4] *The Idylls of the King, The Passing of Arthur.*
[5] James 5:16b.

more weight with God then do shouted petitions.

The power behind prayer is the power of intimacy. *It is the power of a whisper!*

PRAYER

Father, sometimes I am too loud and busy to hear Your soft voice. Teach me the simplicity of silence and the power of a whisper.

PERSONAL REFLECTIONS

Day Twenty-Seven

THE FUTURE IS YOURS

*Words whispered from the pillow of royal intimacy
can literally rearrange the future.*
Finding Favor With the King, 71

———

SCRIPTURE READING

DEUTERONOMY 30:15–20, IN WHICH GOD PLACES BEFORE
THE ISRAELITES THE CHOICE OF LIFE OR DEATH: TO LOVE
AND OBEY HIM AND LIVE, OR TO REJECT HIM AND DIE.

———

D id you note the phrase *"rearrange the future"*? I didn't say "re-arrange the furniture"! An old adage refers to rearranging the deck chairs on the *Titanic* while it is sinking. Do you feel like that is what you often do? The key is distance. The closer you get to him the softer you can speak. The lesson is that those who cultivate intimacy can change their destiny by just a whisper.

In Christ your eternal destiny is sure and secure but the course of your life on earth is not predetermined. The choices you make every day influence your future. Some people insist that there is no such thing as free choice. The prevailing view of modern science is that all life on earth is the product of random forces acting in a closed deterministic system.

Therefore everything we do was predetermined long ago by one "roll of the dice" at the beginning of time. There is no free choice; we have no real control over our lives.

God's Word says otherwise. The Bible is full of people making choices and receiving the consequences of those choices, for either good or bad. Adam and Eve chose to disobey God and were cast out of Eden. Abraham chose to believe God, and his faith was counted to him as righteousness.[1] The rich young ruler, seeking eternal life, chose to keep his wealth instead, and went away sorrowful.[2] The thief on the cross chose to trust in Jesus and His coming kingdom and received the promise of paradise.[3] The choices each of these individuals made affected their destiny.

It is the same with you and me. We shape our destiny by the decisions we make every day. At the same time, however, a lifetime of poor choices can be redeemed by the whispered voice of intimacy in the secret place of communion with the Father. Your destiny is *not* fixed. Your past does *not* predetermine your future. Through worship, prayer, and an intimate relationship with the Lord, you can change your destiny and the destinies of your family, city, nation, and even the world.

God has said, "Come now, and let us reason together. . . . Though your sins are like scarlet, they shall be as white as snow; though they are red like crimson, they shall be as wool."[4] Jesus promised: "If two of you agree on earth concerning anything that they ask, it will be done for them by My Father in heaven."[5] Before the Israelites entered the promised land, God set out before them the choice of life through love and obedience or death through disobedience: "I have set before you life and death, blessing and cursing; therefore choose life, that both you and your descendants may live; that you may love the Lord your God, that you may obey His voice, and that you may cling to Him, for He is your life and the length of your days."[6]

---

[1]Genesis 15:6.
[2]Matthew 19:16–22.
[3]Luke 23:39–43.
[4]Isaiah 1:18.
[5]Matthew 18:19.
[6]Deuteronomy 30:19–20.

You *do* have a choice. You *can* change your destiny. In Christ you are already a child of the King. Your eternity with Him is assured. Your future on earth has yet to be written. Speak to the King from the place of intimacy. Let Him rearrange your future. *The future is yours!*

PRAYER

Father, thank You that by Your grace my past does not pre-determine my future. Rearrange my future. Help me walk with You in such a way that my life on earth aligns with my destiny as Your child.

PERSONAL REFLECTIONS

Day Twenty-Eight

IN SPIRIT AND TRUTH

Worship your way to a place of intimacy.
One well-placed whisper could change your life!
Finding Favor With the King, 72

SCRIPTURE READING

JOHN 4:19–26, WHERE JESUS REVEALS TO THE SAMARITAN
WOMAN THE TRUE NATURE OF WORSHIP AND DECLARES
THAT GOD SEEKS WORSHIPERS WHO WILL WORSHIP HIM
IN SPIRIT AND TRUTH.

Worship is the doorway to God's heart.

We humans are worshipers by nature. God made us that way. In the beginning worship was simple and intuitive. Adam and Eve walked in continual unbroken fellowship with God. Creature acknowledged and honored Creator just as the Creator intended.

Sin complicated this simple picture. Separated from God because of sin, mankind lost the knowledge of both the object and the "how-to" of our worship. We know intuitively that worship brings us into the heart of God. What we no longer know is what constitutes *true* worship. This is why so many people around the world "worship" so many different gods in so many different ways.

When the Samaritan woman raised the issue of worship with Jesus at the well, she gave voice to a question that has preoccupied mankind throughout the ages. What is the "right" way to worship God? She thought worship involved a specific physical place such as a temple or a mountain. Jesus told her that true worship involves not the physical position of the body but the spiritual position of the heart. He said, "The hour is coming when you will neither on this mountain, nor in Jerusalem, worship the Father. . . . But the hour is coming, and now is, when the true worshipers will worship the Father in spirit and truth; for the Father is seeking such to worship Him. God is Spirit, and those who worship Him must worship in spirit and truth."[1]

To worship God in spirit and truth is to worship God in accordance with His nature, His heart, and His will. This means approaching God with humbleness of spirit and purity of heart. Humility and purity are the protocols of true worship. They are therefore characteristic of those who have attained intimacy with the Father. The psalmist says: "Oh come, *let us worship and bow down; let us kneel* before the Lord our Maker. For He is our God."[2] and "Worship the Lord in *the beauty of holiness.*"[3]

If you want to reach the heart of God you must worship your way to intimacy. The Pharisees of Jesus' day thought they could *work* their way to God. They believed that their good deeds and careful attention to the Law gave them an inside track to God's favor. In truth, however, they did not know God at all. This is why Jesus, quoting Hosea 6:6, said to them: "Go and learn what this means: 'I desire mercy and not sacrifice.' For I did not come to call the righteous, but sinners, to repentance."[4]

That day at Jacob's well the Samaritan woman discovered who Jesus was and learned the meaning of true worship. Her new understanding led to a new intimacy with God that changed her life forever. You can

---

[1]John 4:21, 23–24.
[2]Psalm 95:6–7a, emphasis added.
[3]Psalm 29:2b, emphasis added.
[4]Matthew 9:13.

do the same. Worship the Lord in spirit and truth. *Worship your way to intimacy! It will change your life.*

≡

PRAYER

Father, purify my heart. Help me walk in holiness that I may worship You in spirit and truth. Let me worship my way to intimacy with You.

PERSONAL REFLECTIONS

Day Twenty-Nine

RISE TO YOUR POTENTIAL

They weren't looking for perfection.
They were looking for potential!
Finding Favor With the King, 75

SCRIPTURE READING

MATTHEW 4:18–22; 9:9, WHERE JESUS CALLS FOUR
FISHERMEN TO FOLLOW HIM AND BECOME "FISHERS OF
MEN." HE ALSO CALLS A TAX COLLECTOR TO FOLLOW HIM
AND BECOME HIS DISCIPLE.

---

ou have the potential for greatness.
Everybody does. God created the human race to exercise dominion over the created order. He designed us to rule with Him as co-regents of the physical realm. In God's eyes we are all potential princes and princesses. As a loving Father, He wants to see each of us become everything that He has envisioned for us. He wants to see each of us reach our fullest potential.

Do you see yourself as a prince or princess in the making? How about your family and friends? Your next-door neighbor? That homeless person down the street? That annoying colleague at work that you just can't seem to get along with? Do you think of these people as potential "royalty" in God's kingdom?

In the world, we tend to judge by appearances. We are too easily impressed by human credentials and too quick to write off those who fail to measure up to our standards. God operates by a different standard. He judges not by appearance or by present condition but by *potential.*

Consider the apostles of Jesus. Judging from human standards, it would be hard to imagine a less likely group of people to be entrusted with God's work. Jesus called Andrew, Simon, James, and John to be His disciples. These four fishermen were simple, earthy laborers. But don't write them off as ignorant "hayseeds." Fishing was a major business there in those days, and these men may well have been astute, shrewd, and successful businessmen. Nevertheless, they were not the type most of us would think of first as messengers of God's good news. Yet Jesus saw them as more than just fishermen. He saw them as "fishers of men." And that is just what they became.

Matthew was a tax collector. As a "collaborator" with the hated Roman occupation government, he was considered a traitor by his own people. Jesus looked beyond who Matthew was and saw who he could become. As a disciple, Matthew went from writing tax accounts to writing a gospel account of Jesus that became part of God's inspired Word.

When King Xerxes' emissaries went searching for a new queen, they were not looking for perfection. No woman in the kingdom would be "ready-made" for the king's presence. They were looking for *potential.* They sought young maidens who could grow beyond their present circumstances and be made "fit for a king."

In the same way, none of us is "fit" for the King. But He can *make* us "fit." No matter who you are, where you have been, or what you have done, you can still become the person God created you to be. He knows the potential that He has placed inside you. He stands ready to mold and shape you into that person—if you will let Him.

Don't settle for less than God's best for you. Let Him raise you to the level of the potential He has placed in you. *Let Him prepare you for life in the palace.*

———

PRAYER

Lord, I want to reach my full potential in You. I give You control of my life. Make me into the person You want me to be. Prepare me for life in Your palace.

PERSONAL REFLECTIONS

Day Thirty

DON'T FRET THE PROCESS!

*The only way to be transformed and conformed into an
acceptable bride for the king was to submit to the protocols
of the palace—including soaking in the oil!*
Finding Favor With the King, 78

SCRIPTURE READING

JOHN 13:1–17, WHERE JESUS WASHES HIS DISCIPLES' FEET.
WHEN PETER PROTESTS, THE LORD ASSURES HIM THAT
SUCH WASHING IS A NECESSARY PART OF BEING
HIS DISCIPLE.

I*f you want to see the King, you've got to be clean.*
No one enters a royal audience unwashed and wearing dirty clothes.
To do so would be an insult to the king. Esther, as beautiful as she was,
spent an entire year in cleansing and beautifying treatments to prepare
for just one night with King Xerxes. Joseph was summoned from prison
to interpret the pharaoh's dreams. But before appearing in the king's
presence, Joseph shaved and changed his clothes.[1] Even the king's urgent

---

[1]Genesis 41:14.

summons waited until Joseph was presentable.

In the same way, none of us can enter the presence of the King of Kings unprepared. The stench of our sin makes us unpresentable before a holy God. That is why we need the cleansing of the blood of Jesus and the anointing of the Holy Spirit. These elements remove both the stain and the stench of our sin. The soiled garments of our old sinful nature are removed, and we are clothed in the spotless garment of the righteousness of Christ. Only then are we presentable, fit to enter God's presence.

Cleansing must come before anointing. Otherwise the anointing oil will merely mingle with the dirt. The dirt must be removed first. Jesus made this clear to His disciples (and to us) with an unforgettable example. After the Last Supper, on the night before He was crucified, Jesus wrapped a towel around his waist, took a basin of water, and began to wash His disciples' feet. Foot washing was a task assigned to the most menial of house servants. Peter thought it inappropriate for his Lord to perform such a lowly job. And he said so.

"Peter said to Him, 'You shall never wash my feet!' Jesus answered him, 'If I do not wash you, you have no part with Me.' Simon Peter said to Him, 'Lord, not my feet only, but also my hands and my head!' Jesus said to him, 'He who is bathed needs only to wash his feet, but is completely clean; and you are clean, but not all of you.' "[2]

As Peter learned, we must let Jesus wash us and make us clean or else we have no part with Him. He cleanses us not with water but with His precious blood. After cleansing comes the anointing with His Holy Spirit. This process often takes time, a necessary period of waiting and preparation. Before He ascended, Jesus told His disciples to *wait* in Jerusalem until they were "endued with power from on high."[3] What did they do in the meantime? "They *worshiped Him,* and returned to Jerusalem with great joy, and were continually in the temple *praising and blessing God.*"[4]

---

[2]John 13:8–10.
[3]Luke 24:49.
[4]Luke 24:52–53, emphasis added.

Cleansing and anointing are protocols of the King's palace. Worship allows us to soak in that anointing oil. It prepares us for His presence. Attaining the King's presence is well worth the wait. *Don't fret the process!*

═══

PRAYER

Lord, thank You for cleansing me of my sin and anointing me with Your Spirit. Help me worship my way into Your intimate presence.

PERSONAL REFLECTIONS

Day Thirty-One

WAIT ON THE LORD

Sometimes the King makes you wait
just to purify the outcome.
Finding Favor With the King, 80

═══

SCRIPTURE READING

PSALM 130, WHERE THE PSALMIST CRIES OUT FROM THE
DEPTHS TO THE LORD WITH HIS SUPPLICATIONS AND WAITS
PATIENTLY AND EXPECTANTLY FOR THE LORD TO ANSWER.

═══

Waiting for something good is never easy.
We have been so conditioned to instant gratification that we quickly become impatient with any delay in receiving what we desire. If it does not come right away, we begin scheming and searching out other tactics to get what we want. Unfortunately, we often try to do the same thing in our spiritual lives.

Waiting is an inevitable and even indispensable part of our lives as Christians. It is one of the spiritual disciplines that characterizes mature disciples of Christ. Throughout the Bible God promises to hear and answer our prayers. Why then does He often make us wait? Sometimes the King makes us wait just to purify the outcome. There are at least two aspects to this.

First, God sometimes makes us wait in order to *purify our motives.* Many times we ask things of God without thinking through our request or our reasons for asking. Our request may not be in our best interest. It may not conform to God's will. God may have something even better in store for us. All of these are reasons why God may delay His answer.

The more we wait on the Lord, the more opportunity we have to examine our motives, to make sure that we are seeking Him for the right reasons. Not out of a desire for His gifts or His blessings or even His anointing, but simply out of a desire for Him. Sometimes God makes us wait because He wants us to become so hungry for Him that we can hardly stand it. The psalmist wrote, "For a day in Your courts is better than a thousand. I would rather be a doorkeeper in the house of my God than dwell in the tents of wickedness."[1] His motive was pure. All he wanted was to be in the presence of the Lord.

Second, God sometimes makes us wait to force us to depend on Him. He wants to leave no doubt in anyone's mind, including ours, that what has been done is due to Him and Him alone. The children of Israel endured 450 years of slavery and waited through ten plagues before leaving Egypt so that everyone would know that it was God who delivered them. Gideon waited while God pared down his army from 32,000 to three hundred men. That way when they defeated the Midianite army they would know beyond any doubt that God had given them the victory.

Waiting on the Lord is not always easy, but it can strengthen your faith. Seek the spirit of patient expectation of the psalmist who wrote, "I wait for the Lord, my soul waits, and in His word I do hope. My soul waits for the Lord more than those who watch for the morning; yes, more than those who watch for the morning."[2]

Are you hungry for the King's presence? Do you long for His glory to be refueled on the earth? Don't give up! Keep seeking His face and He will answer in due time. *Wait on the Lord!*

---

[1] Psalm 84:10.
[2] Psalm 130:5–6.

PRAYER

Father, teach me to wait on You in patient faith. Help me purify my motives. Let my heart seek only You and Your glory!

PERSONAL REFLECTIONS

Day Thirty-Two

SEEK
THE KING'S HEART

*If you would become a queen,
you must first court the King.*
Finding Favor With the King, 82

SCRIPTURE READING

PSALM 37:3–9, WHICH TELLS US THAT THE PATH TO
FULFILLMENT AND THE DESIRES OF OUR HEART LIES IN
TRUSTING AND DELIGHTING OURSELVES IN THE LORD.

If you want to be happy, seek the heart of the King!

David knew the secret. So did Solomon (although he forgot it late in life). Jesus knew it too and lived by it. The same was true for Abraham and Moses, and for Paul and all the other apostles. All the great men and women of God in the Bible knew the secret. It was living by this secret that made them great. What was the secret? *Personal happiness and fulfillment in life are found in seeking and doing the will of God.* We are at our happiest and are most fulfilled when we are continually seeking the heart of the King.

David was a man after God's own heart who delighted in doing

God's will. Solomon pleased God by asking for wisdom to govern well instead of asking for riches (God gave him both). Abraham and Moses were known as friends of God because their lives were committed to fulfilling His purpose. Paul said, "For to me, to live is Christ, and to die is gain."[1] Jesus Himself said, "I do nothing of Myself; but as My Father taught Me, I speak these things. . . . I always do those things that please Him."[2]

Worldly wisdom insists that happiness is found in "looking out for number one." As usual, this is the direct opposite of heavenly wisdom. Everyone wants to be happy. God made us that way. There's nothing wrong in seeking happiness as long as we seek it in the right way and for the right reason.

Many people want to enjoy the blessings of the kingdom without getting close to the King. It doesn't happen that way. Only as we seek and draw near to the heart of the King will our own hearts be satisfied. The psalmist wrote, "Delight yourself also in the Lord, and He shall give you the desires of your heart. Commit your way to the Lord, trust also in Him, and He shall bring it to pass."[3] We desire what we delight in. When we delight ourselves in the Lord He will give us our heart's desire. *And our greatest desire will be for Him!*

This was the secret to Esther's success. God placed in her the wisdom and the desire to seek not the riches, status, or power of the king but the *heart* of the king. And that's what made the difference. She was not interested solely in reaching the court of the king. Esther became queen because she *courted* the king! The rest of the young women never made it out of the harem.

Do you want to be happy? Then seek the heart of the King. Are you looking for complete fulfillment in your life? Then seek the heart of the King. You were created to be His bride. Don't settle for merely being on the premises of the palace. Don't settle for life in the harem. *Fulfill your destiny! Seek the heart of the King!*

---

[1] Philippians 1:21.
[2] John 8:28b–29b.
[3] Psalm 37:4–5.

===

PRAYER

Lord, I love You. I will delight myself in You above all else. Give me the desires of my heart, and let my greatest desire be for You!

PERSONAL REFLECTIONS

Day Thirty-Three

MORE THAN
SKIN DEEP

*To be welcome in the palace you must learn how
to "walk the walk and talk the talk."*
Finding Favor With the King, 83

≡

SCRIPTURE READING

GALATIANS 5:16–26, WHERE PAUL COUNSELS US TO WALK IN
THE SPIRIT AND THEN CONTRASTS THE WORKS OF THE
FLESH WITH THE FRUIT OF THE SPIRIT.

≡

T*alk is cheap. True character comes from the heart.*

The Broadway musical *My Fair Lady* tells the story of Eliza Doolittle, a coarse, low-class flower girl who is taught to walk and talk like a lady. Her first test comes when she attends a horse race and mingles with the "upper crust" of British society. In both her demeanor and her speech Eliza appears to be a prim and proper lady of refinement and culture. No one is the wiser regarding her true origins. Everything goes well—until the race begins. Caught up in the excitement of the race, Eliza's shallow veneer of refinement falls away and she reverts to her old manner of speech and behavior. Her newly learned refinement is only skin deep.

In the King's court it is not enough to have merely a superficial façade of "proper" language and behavior. The protocols and culture of the King must soak and permeate every pore of our bodies. Esther spent an entire year immersed in learning both the body language and the verbal language of the king's court. Unlike Eliza Doolittle, Esther's refinement was not skin-deep. It filled her through and through until she *became* the queenly person she was trained to be. Her physical beauty was enhanced by a beauty of character. Esther's "walk" backed up her "talk."

Paul was getting at the same idea when he wrote, "Walk in the Spirit, and you shall not fulfill the lust of the flesh."[1] Not even a whiff of corrupt human flesh is acceptable in the King's presence. That is why we can never approach God on our own. The stench of our sinful flesh will bar our entrance. Only the cleansing blood of Jesus and the anointing of His Spirit open the way for us.

Those most welcome in the intimate circles of the King live by the protocols and speak fluently the language of the palace. In other words, they both "walk the walk" *and* "talk the talk." Through worship and daily obedience they continually soak in the anointing oil of the Spirit. As a result, their lives give off the fragrant aroma of the fruit of the Spirit: "love, joy, peace, longsuffering, kindness, goodness, faithfulness, gentleness" and "self-control."[2] This is both the *character* and the *language*—the *walk* and the *talk*—of those who frequent the innermost recesses of the King's house.

God is no respecter of persons, but He *does* play favorites. And His favorites are those who humbly and out of love for Him surrender their own will to take on His character and speak His language.

Do you want to be welcome in the King's palace? Do you want to be one of His favorites? Then cultivate His character. Learn to speak His

---

[1] Galatians 5:16.
[2] Galatians 5:22–23.

language. *Make them more than skin deep. Let them soak into every fiber of your being!*

———

PRAYER

Father, my life is too full of the flesh. I surrender myself to You. Cultivate Your character in me. Teach me to speak Your language. Let my life exude the fragrant aroma of Your courts.

PERSONAL REFLECTIONS

Day Thirty-Four

GIFTS ARE FOR GIVING

*The whole purpose of the anointing is
to prepare us for the King's presence.*
Finding Favor With the King, 85

SCRIPTURE READING

FIRST CORINTHIANS 12:4–13, WHERE PAUL REMINDS US
THAT OUR SPIRITUAL GIFTS ARE GIVEN TO US NOT
FOR OUR OWN GLORY OR ADVANCEMENT BUT FOR
"THE PROFIT OF ALL."

G*ifts are for giving.*
The film *Pay It Forward* tells the story of how one young boy's act of kindness touches the lives of a succession of people. One kind deed leads to another as each recipient "pays it forward" to someone else.

Jesus said that it is more blessed to give than to receive.[1] Yet how often do we act as though His gifts are for our exclusive benefit and enjoyment? We receive the Spirit's anointing to make us fit to be in the King's presence. He gives us gifts so we can give them away as poured-out oil in ministry and service. To hoard a gift or to seek one for our

---

[1]Acts 20:35.

own profit is to prostitute its purpose.

When Philip preached the gospel in the city of Samaria, one of his converts was a man named Simon, who had previously practiced sorcery in the city. Simon had amazed many people with his magic and made quite a name for himself. After Peter and John arrived in the city and imparted the Holy Spirit to the new believers through the laying on of hands, it was Simon's turn to be amazed. He offered them money if they would give him the same power of imparting the Holy Spirit. Peter justly condemned Simon for his greed and selfishness and for thinking that "the gift of God could be purchased with money!"[2]

In contrast to Simon's attitude, Paul said, "There are diversities of gifts, but the same Spirit. There are differences of ministries, but the same Lord. And there are diversities of activities, but it is the same God who works all in all. But the manifestation of the Spirit is given to each one *for the profit of all.*"[3] Our spiritual gifts are not for ourselves but for others. Paul says that we are all members of one body—the body of Christ—and that every member is important. It is when we work together in selfless giving that the body is complete and fully functioning. And it is only in giving freely of our gifts that we find fulfillment. Jesus said, "Give, and it will be given to you: good measure, pressed down, shaken together, and running over will be put into your bosom. For with the same measure that you use, it will be measured back to you."[4]

We become like the one we spend the most time with. If we spend time in the presence of God we will become giving people because He is a giving God. The anointing of the Holy Spirit prepares us for the King's presence because it makes us more like Him.

Don't despise the Spirit's anointing by ignoring or denying it. Don't misuse it by prostituting it for your own selfish purposes. Let the anointing do its work in your life by preparing you for the King's presence and making you like Him. Don't hoard your gifts. *Gifts are for giving!*

---

[2]Acts 8:20.
[3]1 Corinthians 12:4–7, emphasis added.
[4]Luke 6:38.

=====

PRAYER

Lord, forgive me for being selfish with Your anointing. Transform me into Your likeness. Prepare me for Your presence. Help me give freely of Your gifts for the profit of others in Your body.

PERSONAL REFLECTIONS

Day Thirty-Five

WAIT FOR THE BEST

Don't flirt with lower lovers—save yourself for the King.
Finding Favor With the King, 86

═══

SCRIPTURE READING

FIRST CORINTHIANS 6:15–20, WHERE WE LEARN THAT OUR
BODIES ARE TEMPLES OF THE HOLY SPIRIT AND THAT WE
ARE TO GLORIFY GOD IN OUR BODIES AND OUR SPIRITS,
WHICH BELONG TO HIM.

═══

W*ait for the best.*

In recent years the nationwide "True Love Waits" campaign has inspired thousands of young people to pledge to remain sexually pure until marriage. Sexual purity and abstinence until marriage is a major moral and social issue in our culture today. Many young people, including many Christian youth, are confused on the subject. "True Love Waits" has helped clarify the issue for many of them. Aside from preventing unwed pregnancies and sexually-transmitted diseases, abstinence also spares young people the moral guilt associated with inappropriate sexual activity.

Paul said, "Flee sexual immorality. Every sin that a man does is outside the body, but he who commits sexual immorality sins against his own body."[1] We have physical, moral, and spiritual reasons to remain sexually pure. It is important to save ourselves for the marriage partner to whom we will commit ourselves for life.

As Christians, we are also to save ourselves for our King. In this sense, however, we are not talking about sexual purity but spiritual purity. We are to love and commit ourselves to God alone. He deserves and demands our undivided faithfulness. This is what Paul is getting at in the next couple of verses: "Do you not know that your body is the temple of the Holy Spirit who is in you, whom you have from God, and you are not your own? For you were bought at a price; therefore *glorify God in your body and in your spirit, which are God's.*"[2]

Throughout the Bible, and particularly in the Old Testament, unfaithfulness to God is called *spiritual adultery.* Being spiritually unfaithful is as great an offense to God as being sexually unfaithful is to a spouse. God said, "You shall have no other gods before Me."[3] Jesus provided additional insight when He said, "No one can serve two masters; for either he will hate the one and love the other, or else he will be loyal to the one and despise the other. You cannot serve God and mammon."[4]

Everywhere you go you are surrounded by voices and influences that tempt you to trade your faithfulness to God for some lesser pleasures. These may appear quite alluring and appealing at the time, but don't be fooled. Whenever you "flirt with lower lovers," you always end up disappointed because they never deliver what they promise. You were created for the King and He alone will satisfy your deepest longings and desires.

Don't trade your future joy and fulfillment for lesser pleasures now. Wait for the best. Save yourself for the King. Like the merchant who sold all he had to purchase the one pearl of great price,[5] sell out

[1] 1 Corinthians 6:18.
[2] 1 Corinthians 6:19–20, emphasis added.
[3] Exodus 20:3.
[4] Matthew 6:24.
[5] Matthew 13:45–46.

completely to the Lord who loves you and gave Himself for you. The world will entice you with many things, but only the King will satisfy. Don't settle for lower lovers. *Wait for the best!*

═══

PRAYER

Lord, when the things of the world tempt me to stray, help me remember that You alone satisfy. I want to be completely Yours. You are the best, and I will wait for You.

PERSONAL REFLECTIONS

Day Thirty-Six

GET SERIOUS!

Do you realize the King of Kings wants to get serious with you? He wants to take your relationship to the next level!
Finding Favor With the King, 87

≡

SCRIPTURE READING

PHILIPPIANS 3:7–14, WHERE PAUL SAYS HE COUNTS ALL
THINGS AS LOSS COMPARED TO KNOWING CHRIST, AND
THAT HE IS PRESSING TOWARD "THE PRIZE OF THE UPWARD
CALL OF GOD IN CHRIST JESUS."

≡

H*ow serious are you about God?*
Do you desire Him more than anything in this world? Does the longing for an intimate walk with Him burn like a fire in your soul? Are you ready to do whatever it takes to be close to Him, to give up whatever may be required in order to gain Him?

Of course, I am not talking about salvation here. If you have trusted Christ as your Savior you are already saved. You already possess eternal life. I am talking about moving up to the next level, the level of discipleship where you make the Lord your all in all. Jesus said, "If anyone desires to come after Me, let him deny himself, and take up his cross daily, and follow Me."[1] Notice the sequence: self-denial, cross-bearing, and obedience to Christ. In self-denial we lay aside our own will and plans in favor of His. By cross-bearing we identify with Christ daily in His life, death, resurrection, and ministry. Obedience means that we go where He says to go and do what He says to do.

The King of Kings was serious enough about you to die for you. How serious are you about Him? He wants to lift you higher. But are you willing to go? The path to the next level goes down before it goes up. Humility comes before exaltation. James wrote, "Submit therefore to God. . . . Draw near to God and He will draw near to you. . . . Humble yourselves in the presence of the Lord, and He will exalt you."[2]

Paul was committed to this path because more than anything else he wanted to know Christ. This is why he testified: "I count all things to be loss in view of the surpassing value of knowing Christ Jesus my Lord . . . that I may know Him, and the power of His resurrection and the fellowship of His sufferings, being conformed to His death; in order that I may attain to the resurrection from the dead."[3] Paul went down in order to be lifted up. But he always kept the end in sight. He let nothing distract him from his goal: "I press toward the goal for the prize of *the upward call of God* in Christ Jesus."[4]

Are you pursuing the upward call of God? That is where the greatest intimacy is found. Going to the next level means greater sacrifice and greater suffering. But it also means greater blessings and greater glories. When Jesus took Peter, James, and John *up* the mountain with Him, they saw Him *transfigured.* They saw Jesus as He really was. And afterward, they never saw the world in quite the same way again. Jesus took them to a higher level.

What about you? Do you want the Lord to take you to the next level? Go down in order to be lifted up! *Get serious!*

---

[1]Luke 9:23.
[2]James 4:7a, 8a, 10 NASB.
[3]Philippians 3:8a, 10–11 NASB.
[4]Philippians 3:14, emphasis added.

=====

PRAYER

Lord, I want You more than anything in the world! Take me to the next level that I may know You more and be closer to You than I have ever been before!

PERSONAL REFLECTIONS

Day Thirty-Seven

TRUST YOUR
TEACHER!

Listen to the King's chamberlain.
Finding Favor With the King, 90

═══

SCRIPTURE READING

JOHN 14:15–27, WHERE JESUS PROMISES TO SEND THE HOLY
SPIRIT AS A HELPER AND A TEACHER TO ABIDE WITH HIS
DISCIPLES AND TEACH THEM ALL THINGS.

═══

*A*re *you teachable?*

Do you recognize the limitations of your own knowledge and expertise? Do you welcome and even seek out the instruction or training of a knowledgeable and experienced teacher? Or are you the type who plunges blindly and stubbornly on, rejecting advice and counsel, preferring to proceed by trial and error?

Humility is one of the protocols for approaching the King. And one of the characteristics of humility is a teachable spirit. Esther was teachable. Her humble spirit opened the way for her elevation from peasant girl to queen. She knew that she had no clue how to please and win the affection and favor of the king. Esther did not know, and she *knew* that she did not know! This is why she turned to someone who did know—Hegai, the king's chamberlain.

Hegai knew King Xerxes better than anyone else in the palace. He knew the king's preferences, his likes and dislikes, perhaps better than did the king himself. Hegai had knowledge and experience, and Esther trusted his judgment. Esther's teachable spirit put her in the position to rise above all the other virgins in the harem and win the king's heart.

Like Esther, we have a chamberlain, a Teacher to instruct us in the heart, mind, and ways of our King. Jesus promised His disciples, "I will pray the Father, and He will give you another Helper, that He may abide with you forever; the Spirit of truth. . . . But the Helper, the Holy Spirit, whom the Father will send in My name, *He will teach you all things*, and bring to your remembrance all things that I said to you."[1]

The Holy Spirit guides us into all truth.[2] He testifies of Jesus.[3] He "bears witness with our spirit that we are children of God."[4] "With groanings which cannot be uttered" He intercedes for us "according to the will of God."[5] He opens our spirits to receive revelation and to understand the Scriptures. He abides in us and gives us unbroken access to the King. He teaches us how to worship. He fills us, gives us spiritual gifts, and empowers us for the King's service. He conforms us to the image of Christ and produces in our lives the fruits of righteousness.

All of these things—and more—the Holy Spirit does for us. *If* we let Him. *If* we listen to Him.

If you want to find favor with the King, humble yourself as Esther did. Listen to the King's chamberlain. Unlike Hegai, who was merely a human servant of King Xerxes, the Holy Spirit is divine. He knows the heart and mind of the King because He and the King are one. Don't let pride or an unteachable spirit keep you from getting close to the King. The Holy Spirit is a thoroughly reliable and trustworthy Guide. *Trust your Teacher!*

---

[1]John 14:16–17a, 26, emphasis added.
[2]John 16:13.
[3]John 15:26.
[4]Romans 8:16.
[5]Romans 8:26b–27b.

≡

PRAYER

Lord, thank You for giving me the Holy Spirit as my Helper, Guide, and Teacher. Holy Spirit, I humbly submit myself to Your instruction. Teach me the heart, mind, and ways of the King. Prepare me for His presence!

PERSONAL REFLECTIONS

Day Thirty-Eight

WHICH ARE YOU?

God has this incredible idea that church is about Him.
Finding Favor With the King, 94

SCRIPTURE READING

REVELATION 3:1–6 AND 2:8–11, WHERE THE LORD CHASTENS
THE CHURCH IN SARDIS FOR BEING DEAD WHILE CLAIMING
TO BE ALIVE AND COMMENDS THE CHURCH IN SMYRNA FOR
BEING RICH EVEN THOUGH IT IS POOR.

I*f God decided not to show up at your church next Sunday, would anyone notice?*

Would He be missed? Would the congregation immediately enter a time of corporate soul-searching and prayer to find out what was wrong? Or would you go merrily on your way as if nothing had happened?

Many churches continue their routine business week after week, completely unaware that the Master of the house is not even there. It is like attending a party or a great banquet and having a great time but never even seeing or speaking to the host.

This was the problem of the church in Sardis. Christ, the Master of the house, had no words of commendation for Sardis because He found nothing commendable there. He told them, "I know your works, that you have a name that you are alive, but you are dead."[1] No doubt the church in Sardis was very busy. They probably had a full range of ministries and services to their community. Undoubtedly their worship was proper and correct and perhaps even lively and entertaining. They had a good reputation and may even have had money and prestige in the city.

The church in Sardis had the form of godliness, the appearance of life. They thought they were alive and well. The rest of the city thought they were alive and well. After all, they had a *name* that they were alive. Their only problem was that the Holy Spirit had departed, and they never saw Him go. They were dead and didn't even know it!

Contrast this with the church in Smyrna, which received no condemnation from the Lord, only commendation. Of this congregation Jesus said simply, "I know your works, tribulation, and poverty (but you are rich)."[2] Whatever the Christians in Smyrna lacked in material wealth they made up for in spiritual riches. They may have been poor in the things that the world values, but they were rich where it counted—they had the King!

Where does your church fit? Sardis? Smyrna? Or somewhere in between? Even more important, where do *you* fit? God has this incredible idea that church is about Him. Yet so often we try to make it about *us*. We try to turn church into our own private "bless-me" club. Our entire focus centers on how many chills, thrills, and goose bumps we get and how well we are entertained. Rarely do we even *think* to ask what our King wants.

It doesn't matter how big your church is, or how rich. It doesn't matter how many programs and ministries you have. It doesn't matter how exciting your worship is or how eloquent your pastor may be. Without the King, you have *nothing*!

Don't settle for artificial worship and dead formalism, either for yourself or for your church. You have a choice: Sardis or Smyrna. *Which are you? Which do you want to be?*

---

[1] Revelation 3:1b.
[2] Revelation 2:9a.

═══

PRAYER

Lord, forgive me for my artificiality and pretense. Forgive me for those times when I forget that church is about You and not me. Renew my spirit with Your ever-flowing life. Renew my church. May we both reflect the spirit of Smyrna.

PERSONAL REFLECTIONS

Day Thirty-Nine

MIRROR YOUR MODEL

*Seek out someone who has
already been to the inner chambers.*
Finding Favor With the King, 98

===

SCRIPTURE READING

EXODUS 33:7–11, WHICH DESCRIBES HOW MOSES ENTERED
THE TABERNACLE TO SPEAK WITH GOD FACE TO FACE.
WHEN MOSES RETURNED TO THE CAMP, HIS SERVANT
JOSHUA STAYED BEHIND.

===

The best way to learn anything is to see it modeled.

If you want to go somewhere you have never been before, find someone who already knows the way. Someone who's been there. Someone who can tell you where all the pitfalls and false turns are so you can stay on track. Someone whose brain you can pick, whose knowledge and experience you can take advantage of.

Trial and error is okay, sometimes even essential. After all, failure can be a great teacher for someone willing to learn. How much better, though, to shadow someone who has already walked that road. Someone who can say, "Been there, tried that; it didn't work. Here's what you do."

Failure is a good teacher, but experience is better.

Joshua learned early on the importance of a good mentor. He was a man who wore many hats: warrior, commander of Israel's army, one of the twelve spies Moses sent across the Jordan to scope out the land of Canaan. Joshua was Moses' personal servant and assistant. He was also Moses' designated successor.

Moses was Joshua's model. Joshua shadowed Moses wherever he went, serving his needs, carrying out his instructions, and trying to learn everything he could from the great leader. One of the things Joshua picked up from Moses was a deep hunger for God. He knew that any successor to Moses would have to be more than a warrior and an administrator. Above all else he would have to be a man of God who was totally committed to God's will and ways.

Joshua learned how to get close to God by first spending time with Moses, God's friend. He accompanied Moses at least partway up Mount Sinai when Moses was on his way to receive the Ten Commandments from the hand of God. Later, after the tabernacle was erected outside the Israelite camp, Joshua entered with Moses. But when Moses left to return to the camp, Joshua remained behind: "So the Lord spoke to Moses face to face, as a man speaks to his friend. And he would return to the camp, but his servant Joshua . . . did not depart from the tabernacle."[1]

Joshua was in training. He was already skilled as a soldier and a leader. Now he was being trained in experiencing the presence of God. To get to that place of intimacy, he walked beside someone who had been there before him. By the time Moses died Joshua was ready to take his place. Like Moses before him, Joshua knew the inner chambers of the King.

Who do you know and trust that could model for you the kind of life in God you are looking for? Who has been where you want to go and could help you get there? Who can show you how to attain the inner chambers of the King? Find that person and, if he or she is willing,

[1]Exodus 33:11.

stay close at hand and learn everything you can. Let that person model the intimate God-life for you. Then, *mirror your model*!

———

PRAYER

Lord, I want to be intimate with You. Show me someone who can become my model and teach me how to attain Your inner chambers.

PERSONAL REFLECTIONS

Day Forty

IT'S NOT ABOUT YOU

Refuse to prostitute the King's riches for private advantage.
Finding Favor With the King, 99

≡

SCRIPTURE READING

ROMANS 12:1–18, WHERE PAUL SAYS WE ARE TO BE LIVING
SACRIFICES AND USE OUR GIFTS NOT FOR OUR OWN
ADVANTAGE BUT FOR THE GOOD OF THE CHURCH.

≡

*I*t's not about you.

Or me either. It's not about any human individual, and never has been. From the beginning it has always been about God. All of creation exists by His command, and His Word alone sustains it. We humans live by and for God's pleasure and purpose. He created us to house and display His glory. We have nothing that He did not give us.

Yet sometimes we are so quick to take credit for the spiritual graces and gifts in our lives as if they are of our own making. Intimacy and favor with God are wonderful, but they carry a risk. Unless we stay on our guard we can let our favored position go to our head. We can become "proud" of our access to the King and the gifts and blessings He has given us. Before long we begin to presume on our relationship. We begin to act as though the riches He shares with us are for our own personal pleasure and advantage.

God loves each of us as individuals, but His purpose is always larger than the individual. He bestows His gifts for the good and growth of all His people. We have no right to prostitute those riches for our personal use alone.

It is easy to become seduced by the praise or acclaim others may shower on us because of our gifts or abilities. Rather than take credit for them, we should offer them back to the Lord as a sacrifice of praise and gratitude. Paul said that we should offer ourselves as "a living sacrifice, holy, acceptable to God, which is [our] reasonable service."[1] As living sacrifices we claim nothing for ourselves but give ourselves totally to our King.

Rather than boast about our gifts and access, Paul says we should not think more highly of ourselves than we ought but to think soberly.[2] We are to use the gifts and riches we receive from the King for the good of the body of Christ—our fellow believers. Every word in Romans 12:1–18 places the focus of our attention on others rather than ourselves. Paul says, "Be kindly affectionate to one another with brotherly love, in honor *giving preference to one another*."[3] Lest we develop too lofty a regard for ourselves Paul says, "Be of the same mind toward one another. Do not set your mind on high things, but associate with the humble. Do not be wise in your own opinion."[4]

There is no place in the body of Christ for self-seeking or self-promotion. The church has only one Head, and it is not you or me. It is Christ. Nothing we have is our own. We brought nothing into this world and we can take nothing out of it. All we have belongs to Christ, and we must use it for His glory and His alone.

Don't prostitute the King's riches for your own selfish aims. It's not about you. Give yourself to God as an act of abandoned worship—as *a living sacrifice.*

[1] Romans 12:1b.
[2] Romans 12:3b.
[3] Romans 12:10, emphasis added.
[4] Romans 12:16.

≡

PRAYER

Lord, forgive me for forgetting that it's all about You, not me. I offer myself as a living sacrifice to You. Use me as You will.

PERSONAL REFLECTIONS

Day Forty-One

LIVE TO
PLEASE THE KING

We don't succeed by doing what we please.
Finding Favor With the King, 100

≡

SCRIPTURE READING

FIRST SAMUEL 15:1–29, WHERE SAUL DISOBEYS GOD'S
INSTRUCTIONS AND SAMUEL TELLS HIM THAT GOD WILL
TAKE THE KINGDOM AWAY FROM HIM.

≡

What *you* want is not important; what the *King* wants is *all-important.*

Which song best describes your life: the old gospel hymn "Have Thine Own Way, Lord" or the popular Sinatra tune "I Did It My Way"? Do you deliberately seek God's will daily as the guiding principle of your life? Do you take joy in obeying His Word? Or do you always insist on doing things your own way?

Humans have been defying God ever since the garden of Eden. Stubbornly and rebelliously we have insisted on charting our own course. The Bible calls this sin. And sin is repulsive to God, a stench in His nostrils. Sin is a pandemic that infects the entire human race. David wrote, "The Lord looks down from heaven upon the children of men, to see if there are any who understand, who seek God. They have all turned aside, they have together become corrupt; there is none who does good, no, not one."[1] Paul echoed the same thought when he wrote, "For all have sinned and fall short of the glory of God."[2]

Defying God in favor of our own way is always wrong. It is always fruitless. And ultimately it will lead to disaster. This is what King Saul discovered when he failed to follow God's instructions to wipe out the Amalekites completely. Instead of killing every man, woman, and child and destroying all their wealth and livestock, as he was told, Saul spared the Amalekite king as well as the best of the Amalekites' livestock and goods as spoil for the people. This prompted the Lord to declare to Samuel, "I greatly regret that I have set up Saul as king, for he has turned back from following Me, and has not performed My commandments."[3]

When Saul claimed that he had spared the livestock for making a sacrifice to the Lord, Samuel replied, "Has the Lord as great delight in burnt offerings and sacrifices, as in obeying the voice of the Lord? Behold, *to obey is better than sacrifice*, and to heed than the fat of rams. For *rebellion is as the sin of witchcraft*, and *stubbornness is as iniquity and idolatry*. Because you have rejected the word of the Lord, He also has rejected you from being king."[4]

God takes disobedience seriously. He places rebellion and stubbornness in the same category as witchcraft and idolatry. Saul's life displayed an independent streak, a spirit of rebellion that eventually cost him everything, including his life. First Samuel 13:14 reveals that God had already sought out "a man after His own heart" to replace Saul as king. This, of course, was David.

Who are you most like? Saul, obstinately digging in your heels and saying, "I'll do it my way!" or David, passionately pursuing the heart of God? You will never succeed by doing what you please. The path to

---

[1] Psalm 14:2–3.
[2] Romans 3:23.
[3] 1 Samuel 15:11a.
[4] 1 Samuel 15:22–23, emphasis added.

success, joy, and intimacy is found in obedience. Don't live to please yourself. *Live to please the King!*

═══

PRAYER

Father, forgive me for living to please myself rather than You. Help me walk in obedience. I will daily seek Your will as the guiding principle of my life.

PERSONAL REFLECTIONS

Day Forty-Two

· TAKE THE NEXT STEP

*God is no respecter of persons, but He will do some things
for some people that He won't do for others.*
Finding Favor With the King, 103

≡

SCRIPTURE READING

MATTHEW 12:38–50, WHERE JESUS REFUSES TO PERFORM A
SIGN "ON DEMAND" AND THEN IDENTIFIES HIS "FAMILY"
AS THOSE WHO DO THE WILL OF HIS FATHER.

≡

B*lood is thicker than water.*
We all do things for family that we won't do for anybody else.
Familial love trumps all other bonds. Family members have a certain
claim to our favor just because they are family. At the same time, we
usually act more quickly for someone we know well and have a close
relationship with than for someone who is more distant.

When some Pharisees asked Jesus for a "sign," He refused. Why
would a man who widely and openly performed many signs, like healing
the sick, curing the blind and the lame, and even raising the dead, refuse
the Pharisees' request? For one thing, Jesus was not an "on demand"
performer. And these Pharisees were not "family." They had no interest

in Jesus for who He was or what He could do. They were looking for a reason to accuse Him. Jesus told them that the only sign they would receive was the sign of Jonah, a reference to His approaching death.

A few verses later Jesus gave His definition of *family*: "For whoever does the will of My Father in heaven is My brother and sister and mother."[1] He was saying that spiritual "blood" is thicker than physical blood. Spiritual relationships take priority over natural relationships.

Favor comes to those who are willing to draw near. If you want to see God working in your life you must have more than just a passing acquaintance with Him. The closer you are to God, the more His favor will cover you. Favor grows out of relationship. The church, the body of Christ, is also the *family* of God. Even within this family God will do for some what He won't do for others. This is not favoritism; it is *favor*.

The Father loves all His children equally, but His favor rests on some more than on others. Why? Favor is not a matter of earning privileges. In Christ we all have the same privileges and the same access to the Father. Favor is a matter of choosing freely to learn what pleases the King and what His desires are and adjusting our lives and desires accordingly. It comes from drawing near to God not because we want something from Him but because we love Him and genuinely desire to please Him and become like Him. In other words, favor grows from delighting ourselves in the Lord.

We were created to take pleasure in our relationship with God. When we delight in Him—when we truly desire Him above all others— this is when His favor rests upon us. God loves all His children, but His favor rests on those who are willing to take the next step of learning what He wants, adjust their lives accordingly, and delight themselves in Him.

How about you? Do you want to become one of the favored? Then adjust your life around the King's desires. *Take the next step!*

---

[1]Matthew 12:50.

PRAYER

Father, thank You for making me part of Your family. I want to feel Your heart and know Your mind. Help me to love You with all my heart so that I may live for You alone.

PERSONAL REFLECTIONS

Day Forty-Three

TAILOR-MADE FOR HIS RIGHTEOUSNESS

Our King does not alter the robe of righteousness to fit the person. He alters the person to fit the robe of righteousness!
Finding Favor With the King, 108

═══

SCRIPTURE READING

SECOND CORINTHIANS 5:17–21, WHERE PAUL DECLARES
THAT ALL WHO ARE IN CHRIST ARE NEW CREATIONS AND
THAT CHRIST BECAME SIN FOR US THAT WE MIGHT BECOME
THE RIGHTEOUSNESS OF GOD IN HIM.

═══

G *od's standards are nonnegotiable.*
The Lord does not water down His requirements for anyone. He does not "change the rules" from one person to the next. God is unchanging. James calls Him "the Father of lights, with whom there is no variation or shadow of turning."[1] Hebrews 13:8 says, "Jesus Christ is the same yesterday, today, and forever." Whether male or female, young or old, rich or poor, everyone must come to God the same way: through

---

[1]James 1:17b.

repentance and faith in Christ. The ground is level at the foot of the cross.

Many people try to play "Let's Make a Deal" with God. They try to strike a personal bargain with Him on their own terms. They never stop to think that God is under no obligation to deal with them at all. He does so because of His grace. Others treat the Word of God like a cafeteria line, picking out only what they want and leaving the rest. Neither of these approaches gains any ground with God. We must come on His terms or not at all. We cannot choose only the things we like and ignore the others. It is all or nothing.

God will not "dumb down" His standards to our level. Instead, through His Spirit He will raise us up to the level of His standards. We must be righteous before we can enter the presence of the King. But we have no righteousness of our own. When we are born again by the Spirit of God, we receive the righteousness of Christ. We become new creatures fitted for His righteousness. Paul wrote, "Therefore, if anyone is in Christ, he is a new creation; old things have passed away; behold, all things have become new."[2] This new creation reconciles us to God and imparts to us the ministry of reconciliation.[3] He changes us and infuses us with new purpose.

How does this transformation take place? Paul sums it up this way: "For He made Him who knew no sin to be sin for us, that we might become the righteousness of God in Him."[4] Our King does not alter His robe of righteousness to fit us. He alters us to fit His robe of righteousness. In Christ we put off the old man and put on the new man.[5] Isaiah says to exchange "the garment of praise for the spirit of heaviness."[6] A few verses later he says, "I will greatly rejoice in the Lord, my soul shall be joyful in my God; for He has clothed me with the garments of salvation, He has covered me with the robe of righteousness, as a

---

[2] 2 Corinthians 5:17.
[3] 2 Corinthians 5:18–19.
[4] 2 Corinthians 5:21.
[5] Ephesians 4:22–24.
[6] Isaiah 61:3.

bridegroom decks himself with ornaments, and as a bride adorns herself with her jewels."[7]

If you are in Christ, He has given you His robe of righteousness. Don't worry that it won't fit. It will. He is changing *you*. You are being *tailor-made for His righteousness*!

———

PRAYER

Lord, thank You for clothing me in Your robe of righteousness. Alter my heart, mind, and character so that I can wear it well.

PERSONAL REFLECTIONS

---

[7]Isaiah 61:10.

Day Forty-Four

FOCUS ON THE KING!

Ignore man's opinion; seek the King's face.
Finding Favor With the King, 109

===

SCRIPTURE READING

MARK 10:46–52, WHERE BLIND BARTIMAEUS APPEALS
PASSIONATELY TO JESUS AND RECEIVES HIS SIGHT.

===

W*hen you are focused on the King, nothing else matters.*
It's truly amazing how the things of the world that cause us
so much anxiety shrink to insignificance when our eyes are on the
King! Poet Helen Lemmel expressed it this way: "Turn your eyes upon
Jesus, look full in His wonderful face, and the things of earth will grow
strangely dim in the light of His glory and grace."[1] The beauty and
glory of our Lord's face outshine any splendor that this world can
offer.

Jesus was leaving the city of Jericho. A blind beggar named Bartimaeus, when he heard that Jesus was passing by, cried out to Him in a
loud voice, "Jesus, Son of David, have mercy on me!"[2] Many in the
crowd told him to be quiet. They probably thought that Jesus was too

---

[1]Helen H. Lemmel, copyright 1922 by Singspiration Music/ASCAP. All rights reserved.
[2]Mark 10:47b.

busy or too important to be bothered by the likes of someone such as Bartimaeus. So much for man's opinion!

Bartimaeus did not care what others thought. He was determined to get to Jesus and receive his sight. So he simply cried out even louder. Jesus heard his cry and called him over. When Jesus asked what he wanted, Bartimaeus replied, "Rabboni, that I may receive my sight."[3] Jesus granted his request, and Bartimaeus immediately began following Jesus down the road.

If Bartimaeus had heeded the opinion of the crowd, he would never have received his sight. He would have died a blind beggar. But his spiritual eyes were focused on Jesus, and the opinions of others meant nothing.

When David danced before the Lord in reckless and abandoned worship while bringing the ark of the covenant into Jerusalem, his behavior earned him the scorn of his wife Michal.[4] In response to her upbraiding David said, "It was before the Lord. . . . And I will be even more undignified than this, and will be humble in my own sight."[5] When David was focused on worshiping the Lord, nothing else was important, not even his own dignity as the king of Israel.

People will not always understand your passion for the King. They will caution you against becoming a "fanatic," a "holy roller," or a "Jesus freak." "Don't go overboard with this 'Jesus thing,'" they will advise you. Don't listen to them. Ignore their opinions. Fear of people and their opinions will rob you of more blessings than you will ever know. The only opinion that matters is the King's opinion. Don't allow anything to deter you from pursuing the Person and presence of the King.

Don't get distracted by others' ideas or opinions about how you should "behave" before the Lord. Don't let them intimidate you out of seeking His face and pressing in for your blessing. Their opinions don't count. The King's opinion *does*. Keep your focus where it needs to be. *Focus on the King!*

---

[3]Mark 10:51b.
[4]2 Samuel 6:12–20.
[5]2 Samuel 6:21–22.

===

PRAYER

Lord, help me to stop worrying so much about what others think. What You think is all that matters. Give me a holy boldness to seek Your face regardless of the opinions of others.

PERSONAL REFLECTIONS

Day Forty-Five

GOD'S FAVORITE THINGS

Protocol of the Palace #6
If you learn what the King favors,
you can become a favorite.
Finding Favor With the King, 110

SCRIPTURE READING

MICAH 6:6–8, WHICH REVEALS THAT GOD REQUIRES OF HIS
PEOPLE JUSTICE, MERCY, AND HUMILITY.

D*o you know God's favorite things?*
We all have our favorite things: favorite books, foods, movies, songs, Bible verses, etc.

God has His favorite things too. At the top of His list are His children. He loves us. He delights in us. And He will go to any length to demonstrate His love. He proved it when He sent His only Son to die for us on the cross.

Even among His beloved children, however, God has His favorites. They are the ones who commit themselves to learn His favorite things and make them their favorite things as well. As a child of the King you already have the fullness of His love. If you can learn what He favors, you can become a favorite.

So then, aside from His children, what are the King's favorite things? The prophet Micah gives us a clue: "He has shown you, O man, what is good; and what does the Lord require of you but to do justly, to love mercy, and to walk humbly with your God?"[1] Three of God's favorite things are *justice, mercy,* and *humility.*

Justice is one of the great concerns of God in the Bible. The Mosaic Law is full of provisions designed to guarantee fair and equitable treatment for all people. The Old Testament reveals God's particular concern for the welfare of widows and orphans—all the weak and powerless in society who have no one to protect them. God is just, and His favorites among His children are those who are just as committed as He is to justice for everyone.

Mercy is precious because it is such a rare commodity in our world. It is much easier to be judgmental of others than to extend mercy. Judgment can be given from a distance but mercy means we have to become personally involved. The King puts great stock in mercy. Mercy has a reciprocal quality; if you give it out it comes back to you. Jesus said, "Blessed are the merciful, for they shall obtain mercy."[2] He also told a cautionary parable about a slave who received mercy from his master but refused to give mercy to a fellow slave. The master rescinded his mercy to the first slave who was then put in prison until he paid back everything he owed. Jesus concluded with the words, "So My heavenly Father also will do to you if each of you, from his heart, does not forgive his brother his trespasses."[3] The King is merciful, and His favorites are merciful also.

Humility, of course, is a protocol of the palace. It is a passkey to the King's inner chambers. Jesus said, "Blessed are the poor in spirit, for theirs is the kingdom of heaven."[4] Humility is another word for "poor

---

[1] Micah 6:8.
[2] Matthew 5:7.
[3] Matthew 18:35.
[4] Matthew 5:3.

in spirit." The more we realize how needy we are, the more we will take our greatest satisfaction in the King.

Do you want to be one of God's favorites? Then fall in love with justice, mercy, and humility—*God's favorite things!*

———

PRAYER

Father, I want to make Your favorite things my own. Help me to serve justice, to show mercy, and to walk humbly with You.

PERSONAL REFLECTIONS

Day Forty-Six

TO LIVE IS CHRIST

*Our burning passion must be
to fulfill our life purpose in God.*
Finding Favor With the King, 114

SCRIPTURE READING

PHILIPPIANS 1:12–26, WHICH REVEALS PAUL'S PASSION FOR
PROCLAIMING THE GOSPEL, EVEN ABOVE PRESERVING HIS
OWN LIFE, AND WHERE HE SAYS THAT TO LIVE IS CHRIST
AND TO DIE IS GAIN.

W*hy are you here?*
Every life has a purpose. God is a purposeful God. Purpose permeates everything He does. As beings created in His image, we too have a purpose. What's yours? What are you passionate about? What motivates you and gets your juices flowing? Why did God put *you* here on this earth?

Millions of people never find the answers to these questions. Eventually, many of them stop trying. They resign themselves to a mundane and mediocre life of simply trying to make it through each day. Many others claim that there *is* no purpose to life, that life is merely a meaningless evolutionary accident.

God's Word says otherwise. We were created for purpose, and we find that purpose in relationship to the King. Eric Liddell, Scottish missionary to China and Olympic gold-medal-winning runner, said, "I believe God made me for a purpose; for China. But He also made me *fast.* And when I run, I feel His pleasure."[1] Eric Liddell knew his life purpose and pursued it with all his heart—even to his death in a Japanese internment camp in China in 1945.

Paul knew his life purpose also—and it consumed every moment of his life. Even in prison his thoughts were not on his own welfare but that of the churches and the preaching of the gospel. He even saw his imprisonment as serving to help further the spread of the gospel.[2] Paul did not care whether he lived or died, as long as he was faithful to Christ. His earnest desire was that "Christ will be magnified in my body, whether by life or by death. For to me, to live is Christ, and to die is gain."[3]

Torn between two alternatives, Paul finally expressed his belief that he would be released from prison because he felt that his purpose was not yet completed.[4] He still had work to do among the churches and in spreading the gospel of Christ. As far as Paul was concerned, that was his only reason for living.

God has a purpose for your life too. Your destiny may not lie on the mission field. It may not be found behind a pulpit or in any other area of "professional" ministry. God's purpose for your life may lie in the business world. Or in the arts or the sciences. Or in education, law, or medicine. It may even lie on the home front, raising children and building a strong family.

Whatever your purpose may be, find it and pursue it with gusto! The preacher of Ecclesiastes says, "Whatever your hand finds to do, do it with your might."[5] God is not playing games with you. He is not

---

[1]The Eric Liddell Centre, accessed at
http://content.ericliddell.org/ericliddell/content/alifeinspired.htm.
[2]Philippians 1:12–18.
[3]Philippians 1:20b–21.
[4]Philippians 1:22–26.
[5]Ecclesiastes 9:10a.

trying to keep you in the dark about your life purpose. He wants you to find it and fulfill it. That is why He created you.

People with purpose live life with passion.

What is *your* purpose? What is *your* passion? Find them both in relationship with the King. *To live is Christ!*

═══

PRAYER

Lord, help me discover my life purpose in You. Give me the grace and the fire inside to pursue that purpose with passion!

PERSONAL REFLECTIONS

Day Forty-Seven

MOVE THE HEART OF GOD

If you move the heart of God, you move the hand of God.
One nod from God and destiny is altered.
Finding Favor With the King, 114

SCRIPTURE READING

NUMBERS 14:1–25, WHERE THE ISRAELITES REBEL AGAINST
GOD, WHO THEN THREATENS TO DESTROY THEM. MOSES
INTERCEDES FOR THEM AND GOD PARDONS THEM.

Your intercession can move the heart of God!

The Israelites were an obstinate, stubborn people. Ever since leaving Egypt they had done little more than complain and rebel. They had tried Moses' patience (and God's!) more than once. Now on the verge of crossing into the Promised Land, they rebelled again.

Joshua and Caleb, two of the twelve spies Moses had sent to scout the land, were ready to enter immediately and take the land God had promised. The other ten spies, however, threw cold water on the whole affair. They thought the task was impossible. Unfortunately, the Israelites listened to the ten instead of the two. In direct violation of God's command, they refused to cross the Jordan.

For God, it was the last straw. He was ready to destroy the people for their rebellion. Moses, however, stepped in and spoke on their behalf. He reminded God of His patience, mercy, forgiving nature, His mighty acts, and great name. Then Moses concluded with the prayer: "Pardon the iniquity of this people, I pray, according to the greatness of Your mercy, just as You have forgiven this people, from Egypt even until now."[1]

Incredibly, God relented: "Then the Lord said: 'I have pardoned, *according to your word.*'"[2] Moses' intercession moved God's heart, and God moved His hand. God did not destroy the people. Instead, He made them wander in the desert for forty years until every member of that rebellious generation, except Joshua and Caleb, died.

Abraham moved God's heart as well. Just before the destruction of Sodom and Gomorrah, Abraham "negotiated" with Him not to destroy the cities if He found even ten righteous people there.[3]

You might think that Moses and Abraham, both "friends of God," had special sway with Him. The truth is, in Christ we all can have this same access and the same "sway" with God. It is part of our inheritance as His children. Jesus promised, "If two of you agree on earth concerning anything that they ask, it will be done for them by My Father in heaven. For where two or three are gathered together in My name, I am there in the midst of them."[4] James said, "The effective, fervent prayer of a righteous man avails much."[5]

The King listens to those who get close to His heart. He turns His ear especially in their direction. When He smells the fragrance of humility and hears the passionate language of abandoned worship, He moves quickly to respond.

What is on your heart that seems impossible to you? What passionate longing for yourself or for a loved one seems too distant even to hope

---

[1]Numbers 14:19.
[2]Numbers 14:20, emphasis added.
[3]Genesis 18:16–33.
[4]Matthew 18:19–20.
[5]James 5:16.

for? Don't give up hope! In Christ you have access to the Father's heart. Humility and worship will usher you right into His presence. He is waiting, even longing to hear from you. *You can move the heart of God!*

═══

PRAYER

Father, I am amazed that You allow us to move Your heart! Help me draw near to You. Teach me to pray according to Your will and purpose.

PERSONAL REFLECTIONS

Day Forty-Eight

FIFTEEN MINUTES — OR FOREVER?

Favor comes in two flavors.
Finding Favor With the King, 115

SCRIPTURE READING

MATTHEW 6:1–4, WHERE JESUS CONTRASTS DOING GOOD
DEEDS OPENLY TO RECEIVE MAN'S PRAISE AND DOING
THEM SECRETLY SO THAT ONLY GOD KNOWS.

W*hy settle for fifteen minutes of favor when you can have it forever?*

Andy Warhol, twentieth-century American pop artist, once said, "In the future everyone will be world-famous for fifteen minutes."[1] His "fifteen minutes of fame" has become a byword in Western popular culture.

Many people in our society are obsessed with fame and celebrity. They want to know every juicy detail of the lives and loves of the rich and famous. Celebrity magazines sell millions of copies every year. "Tell-

---

[1]"American Masters: Andy Warhol," an article on the program by the same name at *www.pbs.org/wnet/americanmasters/database/warhol_a.html.*

all" books about famous people, written by insiders, routinely make the bestseller lists.

Fame is fleeting. Yet many people consume their lives pursuing it as if it were the most lasting and most important thing in the world. They expend enormous amounts of time, energy, and money trying to capture the praise, admiration, and favor of other people. Yet they give no thought or effort to seeking to please God.

Man-pleasing is a "natural" trait for fallen, sinful human beings. We all want to be liked. Nobody wants to be left out of the group. While obtaining the favor of men may bring immediate gratification, those rewards are short-lived and temporary. Man's favor is as fickle as the wind. You may be everyone's hero for fifteen minutes. But after that, who will even remember your name?

Jesus warned us about getting caught up in seeking the praise and favor of men while neglecting God. He said we should be careful not to do "charitable deeds" just to impress others. Many of the religious leaders made a big show of their good deeds, fasting, and other "religious" activities. They were after the praise of men. Jesus said that was all the reward they would receive.

God's favor is much more important—and much more lasting. Jesus said, "When you do a charitable deed, do not let your left hand know what your right hand is doing, that your charitable deed may be in secret; and *your Father* who sees in secret *will Himself reward you openly*."[2] Of course, it is impossible to *earn* God's favor. He gives it as an act of grace. Our approach to good works reveals the condition of our heart. As long as we seek to please men, we can never please God. Once we set our heart on pleasing God, however, pleasing men becomes unimportant.

Favor comes in two flavors. First is the fleeting flavor of man's favor, which is sweet and delicious, but very quickly goes bland. Then there is God's favor, which is sweeter still and never loses its flavor. In fact, the longer it goes, the sweeter it grows.

---

[2]Matthew 6:3–4, emphasis added.

Which do you want? Your fifteen minutes of man's favor that will never satisfy? Or God's favor *forever* that grows richer and deeper all the time? Don't waste your life pursuing things that will never last. Set your mind on things above.[3] The choice, of course, is yours. Which will it be? *Fifteen minutes—or forever?*

≡

PRAYER

Father, I love You and I want my life to be pleasing in Your sight. Forgive me for trying so hard to please others rather than You. Help me set my heart and mind to do Your will. May all I do bring You pleasure.

PERSONAL REFLECTIONS

---

[3]Colossians 3:2.

Day Forty-Nine

PURSUE THE KING'S PURPOSE

Continual favor flows to those who understand purpose.
Finding Favor With the King, 116

SCRIPTURE READING

PSALM 1, WHICH CONTRASTS THE DESTINIES OF THE GODLY
AND THE UNGODLY. THE UNGODLY WILL BE BLOWN AWAY
LIKE CHAFF IN JUDGMENT WHILE THE GODLY WILL STAND
FIRM AND BE BLESSED.

U*nderstanding your purpose in God is the first step to blessing, favor, and fulfillment.*

Why does God's favor seem to rest on some people more than on others? What is the secret of the "favored few"? It is really quite simple: They have learned that their life purpose is to serve the King's purpose. Personal agendas have no place in the King's court. The King's rule is absolute. His Word is law. To serve any other purpose is to be in conflict with the King.

Jesus said that He came to *serve*, not to be served, and to give His life to ransom many.[1] This was His Father's will, and Jesus lived to do the will of His Father. In other words, Jesus was committed to His Father's purpose. The Father's purpose and the Son's purpose were the same. This is why Jesus enjoyed continual favor. It was not because He was the Son of God but because He understood His purpose and gave himself completely to it: "Most assuredly, I say to you, the Son can do nothing of Himself, but what He sees the Father do; for whatever He does, the Son also does in like manner."[2]

In Jesus' parable of the talents,[3] the servant who received one talent was punished not because he had only one talent but because *he did nothing with it.* The other two servants each doubled their master's money through wise investing. They received blessing and favor because they understood that their purpose was to serve their master's interests. The servant with the one talent was serving his own agenda—avoiding difficulty and inconvenience. Because he did not pursue his master's purpose he received condemnation instead of favor.

God gives us His resources for use in accomplishing His purpose. However, He entrusts them only to those who understand His purpose and are personally committed to it. Understanding purpose leads to walking in it, and walking in purpose leads to blessing and favor. Or at least it *should.* Too often we stop short of *walking* in God's purpose. Instead, we squander our gifts and resources by pursuing our own selfish ends. Then we wonder why God turns His favor elsewhere.

Psalm 1 says that blessing comes to the one who *walks* in the purpose of God—who delights and meditates in His law day and night. "He shall be like a tree planted by the rivers of water, that brings forth its *fruit in its season,* whose *leaf also shall not wither;* and whatever he does *shall prosper.*"[4] This is a description of *continual favor*!

God's favor rests on those who will live for His purpose and no other's. Do you want to flow in the King's favor? Then *pursue the King's purpose!*

---

[1]Matthew 20:28.
[2]John 5:19.
[3]Matthew 25:14–30.
[4]Psalm 1:3, emphasis added.

===

PRAYER

Father, You created me to walk in Your purpose. I lay my personal will and agenda at Your feet. Make Your purpose my purpose also. Let my life be solid, fruitful, and prosperous in pursuing Your interests!

PERSONAL REFLECTIONS

Day Fifty

FAVOR IS FOR DYING

Favor is not the highest accomplishment of life—
the fulfillment of divine purpose is!
Finding Favor With the King, 119

SCRIPTURE READING

JOHN 12:23–33, WHERE JESUS SAYS THAT A SEED MUST DIE
BEFORE IT CAN PRODUCE A HARVEST. HE LIKENS THIS TO
HIS OWN APPROACHING DEATH, WHICH IS HIS PURPOSE
IN COMING TO EARTH.

G*od's favor on your life is not for you. It's for Him.*
You can worship your way into God's favor . . . but why? Why do you want the favor of the Lord on your life? Is it so you can be successful in reaching your dreams? Is it because you want to have "bragging rights" on how good God has been to you? Is it because you want to be on the "inside track" with God so that others will envy you? Or is it because you want to fulfill God's purpose, and you need His favor to do it? Whose mission are you on in life—yours or His?

Jesus was on His Father's mission. He made that clear with every word and every action. The Father's favor rested on Jesus not only so

Jesus could do good deeds and heal people, but so that He could fulfill His Father's purpose. And the Father's purpose was for Jesus to die. Jesus said: "Unless a grain of wheat falls into the ground and dies, it remains alone; but if it dies, it produces much grain. He who loves his life will lose it, and he who hates his life in this world will keep it for eternal life. . . . Now My soul is troubled, and what shall I say? 'Father, save Me from this hour'? But for this purpose I came to this hour. . . . And I, if I am lifted up from the earth, will draw all peoples to Myself."[1]

Jesus' death was necessary for life to flow. He had to die in order to reap a harvest of redeemed souls for His Father's kingdom.

Like Jesus, we are called to die. God's favor is for dying. He gives us His favor so that we can offer ourselves as living sacrifices. Favor is not the highest accomplishment in life. Fulfilling God's purpose *is*. God's purpose is that we die—to sin, fear, self-will, self-rule, and personal agendas—so that we may live in Christ. When we live in Christ we become partners with Him in helping reconcile a lost world to our Father God.

Paul said that we should consider ourselves dead to sin and alive to God.[2] This is the only way we can fulfill our life purpose in God. And it is the ultimate reason why God places His favor on us. When Esther approached the king, unsummoned, to appeal for her people, she was already as good as dead. By law she could have been executed. But Esther had already died to self-will and personal ambition because she was alive to a higher purpose—saving her people from annihilation. This was also God's purpose. When Esther aligned herself with God's purpose, His purpose was fulfilled and life flowed as a result.

Do you want to walk in the purposes of God? Do you want His favor to rest on you? Then be prepared to die. *Favor is for dying!*

---

[1]John 12:24–25, 27, 32.
[2]Romans 6:11.

=

PRAYER

Father, I want to walk in Your purpose. Let Your favor rest on me so that I may die to self and live in You. Let Your purpose be fulfilled in me.

PERSONAL REFLECTIONS

Day Fifty-One

GET READY TO RISE

Whenever God gets ready to elevate you,
He must first introduce an enemy.
Finding Favor With the King, 123

———

SCRIPTURE READING

HEBREWS 12:1–11, WHICH TELLS US THAT GOD DEALS WITH
US AS SONS (AND DAUGHTERS) AND THAT THE RESISTANCE
WE ENDURE PREPARES US FOR GREATER THINGS.

———

E*nemies come in many forms.*
Some are blatant, openly opposing you at every turn. Others are more subtle and devious, appearing as "an angel of light"[1] to entice you away from focusing on God's purpose.

Your enemy may not be a person. It may be a disease that threatens to take your health or even your life. It may be a financial reversal that pushes you to the edge of bankruptcy. Whether large or small, human or otherwise, enemies have one thing in common—they threaten to destroy your destiny.

The appearance of an enemy brings your life to a crisis point. You

---

[1] 2 Corinthians 11:14.

can either capitulate from fear and be destroyed, or you can face your enemy in the power of God and overcome.[2] No enemy can harass you unless God allows it, and if God allows it He has a reason. God's purpose is to bring you to maturity. So if you are facing an enemy, take courage. God is preparing to elevate you. He is getting ready to take you to a new level.

Every athlete knows that bodily strength and stamina develop fastest against resistance. "No pain, no gain." It is the same with our spirit. Resistance forces us to lose our mental and spiritual "flab"—to lay aside every encumbrance and get into "fighting trim." The presence of an enemy propels us into depending on God for strength and victory instead of our own resources.

It says in Hebrews, "Let us lay aside every weight, and the sin which so easily ensnares us, and let us run with endurance the race that is set before us, looking unto Jesus, the author and finisher of our faith, who for the joy that was set before Him endured the cross, despising the shame, and has sat down at the right hand of the throne of God."[3] Jesus faced the enemies of sin, the cross, and the grave. He overcame them and was elevated to the right hand of the Father. His example should encourage us: "For consider Him who endured such hostility from sinners against Himself, lest you become weary and discouraged in your souls."[4]

Because we are sons and daughters of God, He chastens us to mature us. Sometimes our chastening comes in the form of an enemy. Our Father always has our best interests at heart. He turns the resistance against us to our profit "that we may be partakers of His holiness."[5] No chastening or resistance is pleasant at the time, but "afterward it yields the peaceable fruit of righteousness to those who have been trained by it."[6] Facing enemies prepares us for elevation.

Your enemies only *look* big. From God's perspective, they are

---

[2]James 4:7.
[3]Hebrews 12:1b–2.
[4]Hebrews 12:3.
[5]Hebrews 12:10b.
[6]Hebrews 12:11b.

nothing. Once you learn to see them that way they won't seem so intimidating.

Are you pressed about on all sides by enemies and opposition? Hang in there. God is preparing to move you higher. *Get ready to rise!*

―――

PRAYER

Father, sometimes my enemies seem so big! Teach me to see them from Your perspective. When times are tough, help me remember that You are maturing me and preparing to elevate me to a new level.

PERSONAL REFLECTIONS

Day Fifty-Two

DON'T SABOTAGE
YOUR DESTINY

*What you don't eradicate when you are strong will come
back to attack you when you are weak.*
Finding Favor With the King, 125

───

SCRIPTURE READING

JUDGES 2:1–10, WHERE THE ANGEL OF THE LORD CHASTISES
THE ISRAELITES FOR FAILING TO DISPLACE ALL THE
CANAANITE PEOPLES AND DESTROY THEIR PAGAN ALTARS.
IN YEARS TO COME THESE CANAANITES WILL BE A
CONTINUAL PROBLEM FOR ISRAEL.

───

I*gnored problems only get worse.*
It often seems easier to defer a problem rather than deal with it. But that is usually asking for trouble. Ignore a low oil-pressure warning indicator in your car long enough and you may have to replace the engine. Ignore that suspicious lump under your skin for too long and you may have runaway cancer that is extremely difficult to stop. As hard as it seems sometimes, the best way to handle a problem is to take care of it *now.* Otherwise it will come back and bite you.

The Israelites ignored a big problem for so long that they never got free of it. After conquering the land of Canaan, they failed to completely eradicate or evict all the pagan people in the land. Scripture says that after Joshua died, a new generation arose that did not know the Lord. They ignored the lingering presence of enemies in the land. Among these were the Philistines, who produced Goliath, and the Amalekites, from whom descended Haman, the murderous enemy of Esther and her people.

One day the angel of the Lord told them that because of their disobedience in not dealing with the problem, they would suffer serious consequences: "I will not drive them out before you; but they shall be thorns in your side, and their gods shall be a snare to you."[1] And so it was.

You may be in worship or prayer, or in some other season of spiritual renewal and strength, when God begins to deal with you about an issue in your life. It may be an issue of pride or forgiveness; it may involve an addiction, a secret sin, or moral problem. Whatever the issue, the time to resolve it is when God brings it up. If God has revealed it, He wants to take care of it *right then.*

Our problem so often is that we don't like the thought of dealing with our issues. It's painful, embarrassing, and depressing. So we tend to ignore them or procrastinate, telling ourselves that we will take care of them later. But we rarely do.

Unless you take care of the issue from that position of strength when God reveals it, it will hibernate for a time. Then when you least expect it—when you are weak or especially prone to temptation—it will suddenly rear up meaner, uglier, and stronger than before. And then you're sunk!

Don't keep shooting yourself in the foot. Don't keep setting yourself up for continued frustration, defeat, and spiritual mediocrity. As painful as it may be, deal with the issues in your life immediately as the Spirit of God brings you under conviction. Otherwise you will keep fighting—

[1]Judges 2:3.

and losing—the same battles over and over again.

Deal with the problem now. *Don't sabotage your destiny!*

———

PRAYER

Father, it hurts when I have to face who I really am. Give me the grace to be honest with myself and with You. Help me deal with the issues in my life that are holding me back from fulfilling my destiny.

PERSONAL REFLECTIONS

Day Fifty-Three

BREAK THE CYCLE

*Deal with your enemy now or your children will
have to face your enemy tomorrow.*
Finding Favor With the King, 126

SCRIPTURE READING

FIRST CORINTHIANS 15:20–26, WHERE PAUL AFFIRMS THAT
IN CHRIST "ALL SHALL BE MADE ALIVE." CHRIST WILL
"PUT ALL ENEMIES UNDER HIS FEET" UNTIL DEATH ITSELF,
THE FINAL ENEMY, IS DESTROYED.

Everybody is dysfunctional.

Sin has so corrupted our nature and our thinking that we really have no clue what "normal" is. For that we must look to Christ. He is the standard by which "normal" must be measured. Maybe you would object, saying, "Jesus is not 'normal'; He is exceptional." By our corrupt standard, perhaps. But in reality, Jesus is the only "normal" person who has ever lived. In Him we see mankind as God *intended* us to be. Jesus succeeded where Adam failed. His victory over every enemy set the stage for our own victory.

Paul wrote, "But now Christ is risen from the dead, and has become the firstfruits of those who have fallen asleep. For since by man came death, by Man also came the resurrection of the dead. For as in Adam all die, even so in Christ all shall be made alive."[1] We are alive in Christ because He has defeated every enemy—especially death. In the end, Christ, as a faithful Son, will deliver the kingdom to His Father. Until then, "He must reign till He has put all enemies under His feet. The last enemy that will be destroyed is death."[2]

The problem with dysfunction is that it is self-perpetuating. Our dysfunction tends to be reborn in our children, often in magnified form. Let's face it; we pass our hang-ups on to our kids. Whether we call this a "generational curse" or a continuing cycle of dysfunction, it breeds in us and in our children a pattern of frustration, failure, discouragement, defeat, and despair. Unless the cycle is broken somewhere, it will continue to the third and fourth generation and beyond.

Whatever the dysfunctional issues are in your life and that of your family, *you can break the cycle.* The generational curse can end with you. Christ has already defeated every enemy. In Him you can interrupt the pattern of dysfunction that is crippling you. You can break the cycle and leave your children with a legacy of life instead of death, success instead of failure, victory instead of defeat, and fulfilled destiny instead of frustrated dreams.

Who will break the cycle if *you* don't? Unless you break the cycle, your children will have to deal with it. And it may be a much bigger problem for them than it was for you. Do you really want to saddle them with that burden? Let Christ change your "stinking thinking." Allow Him to transform you by the renewing of your mind so that you will know what the perfect will of God is.[3]

You don't have to stay mired in the self-defeating thought and behavior patterns of the past. In Christ you can be set free. And if you become free, chances are your children will too. Don't burden them with a generational curse. *Break the cycle! Today!*

---

[1] 1 Corinthians 15:20–22.
[2] 1 Corinthians 15:25–26.
[3] Romans 12:2.

===

PRAYER

Lord, thank You for defeating every enemy. Thank You for opening the way to true freedom. I'm tired of the continuing cycle of dysfunction. Transform my heart and mind. Break the cycle in me. Let it end here so that my children will be free.

PERSONAL REFLECTIONS

Day Fifty-Four

MORE THAN A CONQUEROR

The size of your enemy is a measure of the size of God's confidence in your ability to overcome.
Finding Favor With the King, 130

═══

SCRIPTURE READING

FIRST SAMUEL 17:1–51, WHICH TELLS HOW DAVID, ARMED WITH A SLING, FIVE STONES, AND THE ANOINTING OF GOD, DEFEATED AND KILLED GOLIATH, A GIANT PHILISTINE WARRIOR.

═══

G od sees potential everybody else misses.

Take David, for example. Who would have thought that a shepherd boy from Bethlehem could bring down a professional soldier nearly twice his height? Or for that matter, could become a king who would lead his nation to greatness? *God did.* When God looked at David He looked beyond the shepherd and saw the heart of a warrior and a king. God knew the potential for greatness that was in David. After all, He had put it there.

Not even Jesse, David's father, recognized the potential in his young-est son. When Samuel arrived to anoint one of Jesse's sons as king of Israel, Jesse did not even call David in from the fields to be in the lineup. One by one the Lord rejected David's older brothers, saying to Samuel, "The Lord does not see as man sees; for man looks at the outward appearance, but the Lord looks at the heart."[1] Finally, David was called before Samuel. "And the Lord said, 'Arise, anoint him; for this is the one!' "[2]

Not long after this God began to elevate David toward his destiny. He brought David face to face with a formidable enemy. With the sol-diers of two opposing armies as witnesses, David brought down Goliath with a single stone from his sling. David succeeded because he knew where his power came from. Just before this battle he told King Saul, "The Lord, who delivered me from the paw of the lion and from the paw of the bear, He will deliver me from the hand of this Philistine."[3]

David also defied Goliath directly: "You come to me with a sword, with a spear, and with a javelin. But I come to you in the name of the Lord of hosts, the God of the armies of Israel, whom you have defied. This day the Lord will deliver you into my hand."[4] Then David brought the giant down with one shot. Goliath never laid a finger on him.

David had a destiny that even he did not know until the day God began to elevate him. God was confident of David's ability to overcome because He knew that David would not trust in his own strength.

God sees great potential in you too. But success never comes without opposition. Realizing your potential will involve overcoming obstacles and defeating enemies. God knows what you can handle because He knows what He has placed inside you. The more you align your life to God's purpose, the more He will begin moving you toward your destiny.

Remember that new levels bring new devils. Don't fear the obstacles and challenges that lie before you. Don't fret over the apparent size and

---

[1] 1 Samuel 16:7b.
[2] 1 Samuel 16:12b.
[3] 1 Samuel 17:37.
[4] 1 Samuel 17:45b–46a.

strength of your enemies. They merely reflect God's confidence in your ability to overcome—*in His power.*

Trust the Lord. He will match your character and strength to the challenges you face. He will make you *more than a conqueror!*[5]

———

PRAYER

Father, I want to fulfill my destiny. Build in me character and faith equal to the challenges I must face along the way.

PERSONAL REFLECTIONS

---

[5]Romans 8:37.

Day Fifty-Five

COME BOLDLY
TO THE THRONE

Preparation trumps permission in the presence of the King.
Finding Favor With the King, 134

═══

SCRIPTURE READING

HEBREWS 4:14–16, WHICH SAYS THAT BECAUSE OF JESUS,
OUR HIGH PRIEST, WE CAN BOLDLY APPROACH GOD'S
THRONE OF GRACE.

═══

God eagerly awaits your visit!

Have you ever looked forward with excited anticipation to the visit of a friend or relative you haven't seen in a long time? It seems as though the day of their arrival will never come. You can hardly wait to see the face and hear the voice of this person who means so much to you.

That is the way God feels about *you*. You are His child, His beloved son or daughter, and He looks upon you with delighted eyes. He loves you more than you can know and loves it when you visit Him.

Is this how you think of God? Do you see Him as a loving Father, welcoming, even eagerly desiring your fellowship? Or do you see Him as a hard-to-please taskmaster, distant and unapproachable?

Unfortunately, this latter view of God is a view much of the church taught for centuries. Some churches still look at God this way. They believe that God is someone you must have special permission to see. Like Haman in Esther's day, they exercise strict control over who has access to the King. Only certain people who fulfill certain conditions can attain the throne room. And who makes that determination? The church leadership.

Fortunately for the church, the Holy Spirit brought renewal through the Protestant Reformation. One of the great revelations in church history was when Martin Luther reintroduced the idea of salvation by *grace*. God became approachable again. People began to see Him more as a loving Father and less as a distant taskmaster.

You don't have to *seek* permission to see the King. He has already granted permission and will never rescind it. The way to God's throne room is free and open to everyone. Jesus said, "Come to Me, *all* you who labor and are heavy laden, and I will give you rest."[1] Of course, there are protocols for gaining the King's presence, such as repentance, humility, passion, and worship. But Christ himself has made all the necessary preparations, and preparation trumps permission every time.

As our great High Priest, Jesus sympathizes with our weaknesses because He was tempted in every way just as we are, yet was without sin.[2] He opened the way to the throne room of God with His blood. And now your Father invites you to a life of intimacy with Him. You don't need special permission. You don't have to go through a human mediator. All you need is a willing spirit and a passionate heart to seek the Lord. That is why the Scripture says, "Let us therefore come boldly to *the throne of grace*, that we may obtain mercy and grace to help in time of need."[3]

In Esther's time of need, she bypassed Haman's strict system of permission and control. She went straight to the throne and received the grace of the king.

---

[1] Matthew 11:28, emphasis added.
[2] Hebrews 4:15.
[3] Hebrews 4:16, emphasis added.

Are you in a time of need? Do you seek the grace and favor of the King? You don't need permission—Christ has already prepared the way. The Father eagerly awaits your visit. *Come boldly to the throne!*

PRAYER

Father, I am awed that You desire fellowship with me! Thank You for opening the way so that I can come boldly to Your throne at any time!

PERSONAL REFLECTIONS

Day Fifty-Six

WILL YOU RISK IT ALL?

Sometimes you must risk everything to become the "very thing" you are supposed to be.
Finding Favor With the King, 135

SCRIPTURE READING

DANIEL 3:1–30, WHICH TELLS HOW SHADRACH, MESHACH, AND ABEDNEGO RISKED EVERYTHING, EVEN THE POSSIBILITY OF DEATH, TO REMAIN FAITHFUL TO THE LORD.

How much are you willing to risk to fulfill your destiny?

Every worthwhile achievement in life involves risk. The business axiom "Nothing ventured, nothing gained" is true for all of life. You cannot learn to swim if you never get into the water. Likewise, you cannot move ahead into your destiny by staying where you are. Many people never realize their destiny because they are afraid to risk anything. How serious are you about fulfilling your destiny? What are you willing to risk?

Shadrach, Meshach, and Abednego risked everything to remain

faithful to God. They refused to worship the golden idol that Nebuchadnezzar, king of Babylon, had set up. Even on pain of death they would not prostitute their faith to follow a false god. Love and loyalty to the God of their fathers was more precious than life itself.

Nebuchadnezzar gave them a second chance. If they would simply worship the idol they would live. Otherwise, they would die. The king arrogantly asked, "And who is the god who will deliver you from my hands?"[1] Shadrach, Meshach, and Abednego chose death over disloyalty. They told the king, "If that is the case, our God whom we serve is able to deliver us from the burning fiery furnace, and He will deliver us from your hand, O king. But if not, let it be known to you, O king, that we do not serve your gods, nor will we worship the gold image which you have set up."[2] The enraged king had them thrown into the fiery furnace.

Where was God during all of this? He was in the furnace with them! Nebuchadnezzar looked into the furnace and saw not three men but four, all unbound and unhurt in the midst of the flames. Nebuchadnezzar described the fourth man he saw as "like the Son of God."[3] Once you dare to risk everything for your destiny in God, you will discover that He is right there with you.

The astonished king called the men out of the furnace and praised the God who had delivered them. He even issued an edict requiring the people to show respect to the God of Shadrach, Meshach, and Abednego. Finally, Nebuchadnezzar promoted them to higher positions of authority in Babylon. When you risk everything for God, He will be glorified even in the eyes of people who do not know Him, and your destiny will be fulfilled.

Risk is scary because there is always the possibility of failure. Such is the nature of risk. Are you willing to risk everything to fulfill your destiny? Are you willing to trust that the God who walked in the furnace with Shadrach, Meshach, and Abednego will also walk with you as you

---

[1]Daniel 3:15b.
[2]Daniel 3:17–18.
[3]Daniel 3:25.

pursue your destiny? How far will you go to follow God? How far will you go to see your destiny fulfilled? *Will you risk it all?*

———

PRAYER

Lord, risk is scary, but I know I am secure as long as I am walking in Your will. Increase my faith, and grant me the courage to risk everything to become the "very thing" I am supposed to be.

PERSONAL REFLECTIONS

Day Fifty-Seven

HONOR THE
BODY OF CHRIST

The collective aroma of humility from many
is more powerful than that of an individual.
Finding Favor With the King, 136

≡

SCRIPTURE READING

PSALM 133, WHICH LIKENS THE UNITY OF GOD'S PEOPLE
TO THE PRIESTLY ANOINTING AND IDENTIFIES IT AS A SIGN
OF SPIRITUAL LIFE.

≡

N*o force on earth is more powerful than the people of God united in
worship and prayer!*

This is why Satan hates and fears the church so much. He knows
that nothing can stand against the power that is unleashed by believers
unified in love and faith. Satan also knows that if he can divide believers he can dilute that power and diminish the church's effectiveness in
the world. Jesus said that a house divided against itself cannot stand.[1]
Although He was answering critics who claimed that He cast out

---

[1]Matthew 12:25.

demons by the power of the devil, His statement applies to the church just the same.

How important is the church to you? What value do you place on regular, active involvement with a local fellowship of believers? Jesus established His church as a *body* for good reason: He knew that there is strength in numbers. The corporate nature of the church is also intended to reflect the unity that exists in the Godhead.

Esther understood the strength and power in numbers. She also recognized the tremendous spiritual power of corporate worship, fasting, and prayer. That is why she asked Mordecai to get all the Jews in the capital city of Susa to pray and fast for three days before she went in to see King Xerxes while she and the maidens with her did the same. Esther knew that the collective aroma of unified worshipers would move the heart of God more than her prayers alone.

A spirit of unity is a sign of spiritual life in a church. It is also evidence of the anointing of God on that body. David wrote, "Behold, how good and how pleasant it is for brethren to dwell together in unity! It is like the precious oil upon the head. . . . It is like the dew of Hermon, descending upon the mountains of Zion; for there the Lord commanded the blessing—life forevermore."[2]

Each of us as individual Christians carry the anointing of God on our lives. When we come together in unity, however, our corporate anointing is greater than the sum of our personal anointings as individuals. In the Bible, the anointing oil often symbolizes the Spirit of God. And where the Spirit of God is, there is life. Where the Spirit of God is, there is power. Where the Spirit of God is, there are transformed lives. Where the Spirit of God is, there is liberty. Where the Spirit of God is, there is unity. Where the Spirit of God is, there destiny is fulfilled.

I don't know about you, but I love the church. I hope and pray that you do too. Don't neglect the body of Christ. There is power in numbers. There is strength in numbers. There is encouragement in numbers.

---

[2]Psalm 133:1–3.

There is wisdom in numbers. There is safety in numbers. There is protection from error in numbers.

Don't try to go it alone. *Honor the body of Christ!*

=====

PRAYER

Lord, I love Your church. Help me to love it more. May my life be a force for unity, not division, for life, not death.

PERSONAL REFLECTIONS

Day Fifty-Eight

SPEND YOUR FAVOR WISELY

She was going to spend her favor to purchase her destiny.
Finding Favor With the King, 137

SCRIPTURE READING

JOSHUA 2:1–15, WHERE RAHAB CHOOSES TO PURCHASE A
FUTURE FOR HERSELF AND HER FAMILY WITH THE NATION
OF ISRAEL RATHER THAN FACE CERTAIN DEATH IN JERICHO.

W*hat would you do to ensure your family's future?*
If you saw disaster looming on the horizon, how far would you go to save your loved ones? I'm sure that any one of us would do whatever was necessary to protect the ones we love. No price would be too high to pay to guarantee that they lived to fulfill their destiny, not even our own death.

When Esther chose to go to King Xerxes unannounced she knew it might cost her life. Yet she regarded her own life as a small price to pay for the salvation of her people. When the crisis came, Esther used her relationship of love and intimacy with the king to her advantage. She spent her favor to buy the lives of all the Jews in the empire, including her own.

Rahab was another who put everything on the line for her family. Like all the other residents of Jericho, she knew about the Israelites who were camped just on the other side of the Jordan River. She had heard of their God and all the mighty deeds He had done on their behalf. She realized it was only a matter of time before the Israelites crossed the river and conquered her city. Rahab wanted to save her family.

One day two Israelite spies came to her door. Rahab immediately saw her opportunity and seized it. Instead of turning them in, she hid them from the men who were looking for them. Rahab now had favor with the two spies, and she was quick to spend it: "Now therefore, I beg you, swear to me by the Lord, since I have shown you kindness, that you also will show kindness to my father's house . . . and spare my father, my mother, my brothers, my sisters, and all that they have, and deliver our lives from death."[1] Rahab saw that Jericho had no future, and she didn't want it to be the same way with her family.

It is interesting that Rahab did not mention herself in her request. Although this was certainly implied, it reveals something of her selfless character. There was more than simple pragmatism at work here. The seed of faith in Israel's God had already sprouted in her heart. She wanted to align herself with Him and bring her entire family with her.

The Israelite spies agreed with her request, and the rest is history. Jericho fell and all the inhabitants of the city died except for Rahab and her family, who joined the camp of Israel. Rahab spent her favor with the spies to buy life for herself and her family, not just physical life but spiritual life as well. Through her marriage to an Israelite named Salmon, Rahab became an ancestor of David and later of Jesus Christ himself. *Not bad for a former harlot!*

Don't spend your favor only on yourself. Don't waste it on things that lead to death. There is too much at stake. Favor is for bringing life and fulfilling destiny. *Spend your favor wisely!*

---

[1]Joshua 2:12–13.

===

PRAYER

Father, Your favor is sweet, but I know it is not for me alone. I don't want to hoard it. Give me the wisdom to use it wisely to ensure a future and a destiny for myself and my family.

PERSONAL REFLECTIONS

Day Fifty-Nine

THE BATTLE
IS THE LORD'S

*Once you are in the King's presence,
the battle is virtually over!*
Finding Favor With the King, 138

━━━

SCRIPTURE READING

SECOND CHRONICLES 20:1–20, WHERE KING JEHOSHAPHAT
BRINGS THE THREAT OF AN ENEMY BEFORE THE LORD.
THE LORD ASSURES HIM THAT HE WILL FIGHT THE
BATTLE FOR THEM.

━━━

The King has already fought and won your battles.

Don't you get tired of the daily battles and struggles of life? I know I do. It seems as though we are always facing a fresh problem or a new enemy of some kind. No sooner do we deal with one than another jumps into the fray to take its place. Spiritual warfare is an unavoidable part of the Christian life. And although God uses our battles to build our character and bring us to maturity, the process is rarely pleasant.

Fortunately for us, our King is also a mighty warrior, so we don't have to face our battles alone. In fact, He has already won them. Our problem is that our human weakness often makes claiming the victory and making it our own difficult.

The King may be a warrior, but there is peace in His inner chambers.

Every soldier needs periodic times of R and R—a safe harbor where he or she can find peace and rest for a while. For believers, this means drawing near to the heart of God, retreating into His inner chambers where there is always peace and rest. It is here, in the place of worship and intimacy, where our battles are either won or lost *before* we even wage them. As I said in *Finding Favor With the King,* most of our battles are waged outside the court (137).

When we move into the King's inner court we leave our weapons and armor behind. We may need them on the battlefield, but they are unnecessary in the presence of the King. When we worship our way into the King's presence He takes up our battles and wins them for us.

Jehoshaphat, the king of Judah, had a problem. A formidable army was on its way to attack the kingdom of Judah. He went before the people, humbled himself, and worshiped the Lord. He laid out the situation, then appealed for God's help: "O our God, will You not judge them? For we have no power against this great multitude that is coming against us; nor do we know what to do, but our eyes are upon You" (2 Chronicles 20:12).

Jehoshaphat worshiped his way into the inner chambers of intimacy with the Lord. In response, God told the king to take his army and go out to meet the enemy. He added, "You will not need to fight in this battle. Position yourselves, stand still and see the salvation of the Lord, who is with you."[1] The king sent singers ahead of his army. As soon as they began singing praises to the Lord, God set the enemy armies against each other and they destroyed themselves. This battle was won in the place of worship.

The same God who fought for Jehoshaphat will also fight for you. Don't fear the conflict, because you are not alone. Worship your way into His inner chambers and wait on Him. *The battle is the Lord's!*

---

[1] 2 Chronicles 20:17a.

PRAYER

Lord, thank You for fighting my battles. Teach me to rest in Your presence and in the reality of victory.

PERSONAL REFLECTIONS

Day Sixty

RISK THE GOOD AND REAP THE BEST

Esther risked *her favor to achieve her purpose.*
Finding Favor With the King, 139

═══

SCRIPTURE READING

MATTHEW 19:16–30, WHERE THE RICH YOUNG RULER
PROVES UNWILLING TO RISK ALL HE HAS TO FOLLOW
CHRIST, AND WHERE JESUS PROMISES THE GREATEST GIFT
OF ALL—ETERNAL LIFE—FOR ALL WHO *WILL* RISK
EVERYTHING FOR HIM.

═══

O*nce you know your purpose, everything else is expendable.*
Discovering your purpose in life will change how you look at all your circumstances. The entire focus of your life will change. Things you once thought critical for your success suddenly become insignificant, especially if they don't advance your life purpose.

Purpose brings passion. Passion will propel you to cast off anything that hinders you from achieving your purpose. It is like stock-car racers stripping their cars of any extraneous items that only add weight and slow them down. Or athletes who shed every unnecessary pound to give them the competitive edge that will help them excel.

Jesus told of a man who found a treasure buried in a field, sold everything he owned, and bought the field, as well as a merchant who found one pearl of surpassing value, sold everything he had, and bought it.[1] These men risked everything for the chance of obtaining something of much greater value.

One man Jesus encountered was unwilling to risk it all, even for something better. The rich young ruler knew his life purpose; he sought eternal life. When he found out what it would cost, however, he was unwilling to pay the price. He went away sorrowful, his destiny unfulfilled and his life purpose forsaken.[2]

In the light of this encounter Peter asked, "See, we have left all and followed You. Therefore what shall we have?"[3] Jesus answered that the Twelve would sit on twelve thrones and judge the twelve tribes of Israel. Then He added, "And everyone who has left houses or brothers or sisters or father or mother or wife or children or lands, for My name's sake, shall receive a hundredfold, and inherit eternal life."[4]

No matter where you are now, the Lord is calling you to a greater and higher purpose. Even if you have found your purpose and are pursuing it, you need to keep pressing deeper and rising higher. Life is a journey, a continual progressing toward the high calling of God. And no matter how much you may have right now, it cannot compare to what awaits you in the Father's house. So hold on to it lightly.

It is so tempting to simply bask in the favor of the Lord and stop there. God's favor is not static; He does not give it for its own sake. His favor is to help you rise to your full potential and achieve your life purpose. He also wants you to bring others along with you.

Esther risked her favor and achieved her purpose—the salvation of her people. She brought all the Jews in the empire with her into a new future full of hope and potential.

---

[1]Matthew 13:44–46.
[2]Matthew 19:16–22.
[3]Matthew 19:27.
[4]Matthew 19:29.

What life purpose has God revealed to you? Will you risk your favor to fulfill your purpose? *Risk the good and reap the best!*

≡

PRAYER

Lord, help me not to get so caught up in enjoying Your favor that I stop pursuing Your purpose. May I be willing to risk the good in order to reap the best.

PERSONAL REFLECTIONS

Day Sixty-One

WHEN RELATIONSHIP SURPASSES PROTOCOL

There comes a point at which relationship will surpass protocol, but don't try it until you have learned the protocol of His presence.
Finding Favor With the King, 139

═══

SCRIPTURE READING

LUKE 18:17, WHERE JESUS TOLD THE SHOCKED RELIGIOUS
TEACHERS AND ADULT KNOWLEDGE-SEEKERS ASSEMBLED
AROUND HIM TO BECOME LIKE LITTLE CHILDREN
BECAUSE CHILDREN POSSESSED THE KEY TO
RECEIVING GOD'S KINGDOM.

═══

Make sure your idea of intimacy with God matches His ideas about it. (*Hint:* Often we find that the more "grown up" we get, the less intimate we become with the God who prizes childlike love above grown-up seriousness.)

From our first day at school, we begin to learn *protocol:* "No talking. Follow in a single line behind the teacher. Do not chew gum. No pushing or shoving. Boys, be nice. In the lunchroom take only one napkin, and make sure you clean up after yourselves."

Then we learn the protocol of relationships. "Smile when you are introduced, extend your hand in a friendly manner and deliver a firm but comfortable handshake. Girls, do not flirt. Boys, do not smirk. Look them in the eye with confidence but not haughtiness. When you part, mention their name again as you bid them good-bye."

Whether it is our first job, first elected office, or the exchange of wedding vows at the altar, the protocols of our functions can be overwhelming. Many of them are dropped once the "new" wears off.

In contrast, our *relationships* possess the power to go beyond the bounds of protocol when genuine intimacy is present.

President Abraham Lincoln's son often irritated the stuffy White House staff members and military brass with his privileged invasions of the Oval Office. They were jealous of his son's intimate approach and at-ease relationship with his father.

The same criticisms were leveled at President John F. Kennedy's son, John Jr., who liked to peer out from under the presidential desk in the Oval Office. This perfectly illustrates the quote from *Finding Favor With the King*:

> *There comes a point at which relationship will surpass protocol,* but don't try it until you have learned the protocol of His presence. (139)

Proximity is easily mistaken for intimacy, but it is not the same. The adults clustered around Jesus had invested days, weeks, or even years following the Lord's ministry. They probably felt a measure of intimacy with their "Teacher." Something happened when children who were meeting Jesus for the first time were honored and welcomed so lovingly by Jesus. He told the adults they *all* needed to be like those children, effectively removing their pride over proximity, and placing the greatest emphasis on intimacy.

Protocol provides important outward stepping-stones or formal approaches to the throne of God. They may be useful in building proper respect and honor for a holy God, but childlike love is the key to His heart.

Esther honored the protocol of the palace in every respect. Even her dangerous attempt to approach the throne was made according to the rules of the kingdom. Yet *it was her relationship to the King* in the end that suspended the mandatory death sentence that protocol demanded.

═══

PRAYER

Lord, I will gladly follow every protocol You lay down in Your Word if it means I can draw near to You. But I am overjoyed by the privilege You've given me to cry out anytime, day or night: "Abba, Father! Daddy, I love You. I need You. I worship You!"

PERSONAL REFLECTIONS

Day Sixty-Two

WHEN RELATIONSHIP SURPASSES PRESUMPTION

*There is a fine boundary between
intimate familiarity and casual presumption.*
Finding Favor With the King, 139

═══

SCRIPTURE READING

MATTHEW 7:22–23, WHERE JESUS WARNS US THAT MANY
WHO CALL HIM "LORD, LORD" WON'T ENTER THE
KINGDOM OF HEAVEN, EVEN IF THEY PROPHESIED, CAST
OUT DEMONS, AND PERFORMED MIRACLES IN HIS NAME.

═══

V isit any country with a monarchy and you will find two primary kinds of people clustered around the king or queen. Both sets of people know how to dress for appearances before royalty, and both groups know how to speak, approach a monarch, and avoid the "never-do" list common to every place or seat of power and authority.

The first group of people typically are proud of their hard-earned achievements. They've stood the test of scrutiny and passed the examinations common in any environment ruled by protocol. In fact, virtually every nation employs "protocol specialists" who accompany the heads of state and key diplomats. The specialists' sole mission in life is to help their nation's leader tread safely through the minefields of ever-changing international and cultural protocol.

The second group didn't necessarily "earn" their position in the royal court—they were *born* to it. They enjoy a *relationship* with their national sovereign that no amount of protocol or proper political positioning can produce. They are *family*.

For this reason, they can do things that would get even the most highly placed protocol-driven diplomat or dignitary into deep trouble. This is true even in the White House.

No diplomat, cabinet head, or congressional leader could enter the Oval Office and begin playing under the president's desk, or lead the President to a toy store display window to point out a desired birthday present. Yet a child, teenager, or spouse can have direct and intimate contact with the leader of the most powerful nation on the planet *as long as they have the privileged access* available only to close family members.

These privileged people also enjoy the *full protection* and *provision* enjoyed by the president. The children and spouses of U.S. presidents receive round-the-clock Secret Service protection for as long as it is necessary—even after that president has left office. (Our Leader, the King of Kings and Lord of Lords, will *never* leave office or lose His power.)

The greatest danger for Christians who focus on protocol while neglecting relationship is that they may cross the fine boundary between intimate familiarity and casual presumption. This is what Jesus described in Matthew 7:22–23—people who "performed miracles" in Jesus' name but wanted to "live life *their* way" (a simple definition of "lawlessness") instead of loving and following Christ in *The Way*. Presumption seeks the *benefits* of His presence. True intimacy seeks Him, not merely the benefits, perks, or power associated with His name and title.

Casual presumption offends God, even if we shout out the loudest in public meetings, "Lord, Lord!"

=

PRAYER

Lord, I'm thankful for every promise and provision You have given to me, but I want more. I want You. I appreciate every gift and privilege You grant to me and those I love, but above all I appreciate You and Your unconditional love for me. I could never earn or deserve the right to fellowship personally with You—but You gave it freely. Thank You, Lord.

PERSONAL REFLECTIONS

Day Sixty-Three

RESIGNED TO THE ABSOLUTE FAITHFULNESS OF GOD

Sometimes purpose requires that you resign yourself to the absolute faithfulness of God.
Finding Favor With the King, 140

═══

SCRIPTURE READING

LUKE 1:46–55, WHERE MARY RESIGNED HERSELF TO GOD'S
ABSOLUTE FAITHFULNESS AND SURRENDERED TO HIS
PURPOSES—EVEN THOUGH SHE DIDN'T KNOW WHY OR HOW
THE THINGS SPOKEN BY THE ANGEL WOULD COME TO PASS.

═══

At some time in your life, you may find yourself in Mary's position. Faced with a situation few if any can understand, and armed only with a word from the Lord, you will have to choose:

A. Will you embrace God's purposes along with the *unknown consequences of your obedience*; or

B. Will you decline the uncertainty of the unknown and seek comfort in the seemingly "less risky" environment of life *outside* of God's purposes?

The Bible tells us that "without faith it is impossible to please Him [God]."[1] It seems that faith is the "currency" of God's kingdom on earth. By biblical definition, "Faith is the substance of things hoped for, the evidence of things not seen."[2]

In the fullness of time, the young Jewish virgin named Mary made a fateful decision to risk all in response to the words of the Lord. She decided to resign herself to the faithfulness of God in the face of the unknown. She declared to the angel of the Lord, "Let it be to me according to your word,"[3] and the result changed human history and fulfilled the highest divine destiny of all time.

Another young Jewish woman named Esther faced a fateful choice between what seemed to be certain death at the hands of Persian bodyguards and *possible* deliverance by the hand of the Invisible God.

Would she choose the false safety of passive observance and watch as her people were systematically hunted down, or would she take the active path of obedience in the face of clear danger and possibly save her people?

Mordecai reminded Esther that while obedience often has unpleasant consequences, *disobedience always has dire consequences* connected to it. He warned her that even if she was silent, God would save His people some way, but it wouldn't help her and her family. Esther resigned herself to God's faithfulness and faced death to preserve life.

What about you? Are you tempted to step back, hole up, or remain silent in the face of a difficult challenge in your life—when you somehow *know* you were born to do *more*?

Each time you find yourself in a crisis or situation that is beyond what you can "fix" or handle on your own, you have a perfect opportunity to lean upon the One who loves to save, heal, and deliver His

---

[1] See Hebrews 11:6.
[2] Hebrews 11:1.
[3] Luke 1:38b.

children. Following Christ in this life is a faith action from beginning to end.

It takes faith to receive Christ as Lord and Savior, and it takes faith to trust Him with family members, daily challenges, business or job-related needs, and provision in times of crisis.

=====

PRAYER

Lord, You know that I have questions and concerns about the future, and whether or not things will work out in the problem areas I've told You about. I often wonder how You will fulfill Your promises and purpose in my life, but now I realize that sometimes Your purpose in my life requires me to resign myself to Your absolute faithfulness. I trust You, even when facing the unknown possibilities of tomorrow.

PERSONAL REFLECTIONS

Day Sixty-Four

LEARN TO WORSHIP WITH YOUR ENEMY (BUT KEEP YOUR EYES ON THE KING)

You have the same choices Esther did the day she prepared a banquet for her husband, King Xerxes, and her new enemy, powerful Prime Minister Haman. She could either focus on the problem or focus on the solution.

Finding Favor With the King, 142

===

SCRIPTURE READING

SECOND CHRONICLES 20:12B, WHERE KING JEHOSHAPHAT AND JUDAH WERE IN DANGER OF DESTRUCTION, AND THE KING PRAYED, "WE HAVE NO MIGHT AGAINST THIS GREAT MULTITUDE THAT IS COMING AGAINST US; NOR DO WE KNOW WHAT TO DO, BUT OUR EYES ARE UPON YOU."

===

We discover the true measure of our faith in God when things go wrong in life. We feel things are at their worst when enemies we didn't know we had suddenly come against us with unreasoning hatred or animosity.

Many Christians seem to freeze or back up when faced with adversity, animosity, or a seemingly impossible situation, but it doesn't have to be that way. You have another and better choice in every bad situation. Learn how to worship God even in the presence of your "enemies" (whether you are confronted by flesh-and-blood opponents or difficult circumstances).

In today's Scripture reading, King Jehoshaphat and Judah faced catastrophe—they were surrounded and outnumbered by their enemies. The king spread out the written threats before God in the temple. Then he prayed a perfect model prayer for anyone who doesn't know what to do. He basically said, "Lord, this one's too big for us. We don't know what to do, but our eyes are on You!" That is the art of worshiping in the presence of your enemy while keeping your eyes on the King.

King David declared, "You prepare a table [a feast] before me in the presence of my enemies."[1]

What a picture! It virtually matches Queen Esther's situation when she prepared an intimate dinner to be shared with her husband, the king, and with the most dangerous human enemy her people had ever faced.

Esther solved the problem with supernatural grace—she learned how to worship in the very presence of her enemies. She had eyes only for the king, so the unwelcome guest was forced to merely observe in envy as she fully enjoyed and utilized her intimate relationship with her husband.

Haman had no idea that his aspirations for greatness by association with King Xerxes were doomed by Esther's unconditional devotion to the king. Intimacy always trumps protocol and political positioning.

Queen Esther didn't make a formal petition to Persia's ruler. She sat next to her most spiteful enemy and drew near to the king in intimate and loving relationship. So King Xerxes drew nearer to her. He was moved to grant Esther her very heart's desire! King Xerxes' words to

---

[1]Psalm 23:5a.

Esther represented everything Haman wanted to hear, but never would:
"What is your petition, Queen Esther? It shall be granted you. And
what is your request? Even to half of the kingdom it shall be done."[2]

———

PRAYER

*Lord, it seems as if I can't get away from the enemies in
my life. They seem to invade my meals, my rest, and my every
waking moment. But today I've made up my mind. I will
worship You and keep my eyes on You—even in the presence
of my enemies. I don't know what to do, but I put all of my
trust in You!*

PERSONAL REFLECTIONS

---

[2]Esther 7:2b NASB.

Day Sixty-Five

WHEN THE KING MAKES YOUR BATTLE HIS BATTLE

Protocol of the Palace #7
If your enemy is the King's enemy,
then your battle is the King's battle.
Finding Favor With the King, 144

━━━

SCRIPTURE READING

ACTS 4:29–30, WHERE PETER AND JOHN, IMMEDIATELY
AFTER BEING ARRESTED AND BEATEN BY THE TEMPLE
GUARDS AT THE ORDER OF THE HIGH PRIEST AND THE
SANHEDRIN, PRAYED WITH THEIR COMPANIONS THAT GOD
WOULD CONSIDER THEIR ENEMIES AND "LOOK ON THEIR
THREATS, AND GRANT TO YOUR SERVANTS THAT WITH ALL
BOLDNESS THEY MAY SPEAK YOUR WORD."

━━━

How many times do we ask God to intervene and fight for us in situations that we created on our own? We fail to pay our taxes on time and then ask God to deliver us from the consequences, or we neglect our marriage relationship and then ask Him to step in and salvage the mess that we created. In His great mercy, He often does help us in those situations. However, it is much better to align our lives with His purposes and then enjoy the "consequences" of obedience and relationship with the King!

Queen Esther was focused on obeying Mordecai's counsel and fulfilling her purpose "for such a time as this." In the process, she found herself face to face with an overpowering enemy who was poised to destroy what God had created by covenant promise. The Jews were descendants of Abraham, a man whose descendants had been blessed by God. By divine design, Esther had come into a covenant relationship with King Xerxes as his queen, so Esther's mortal enemy automatically became the sworn enemy of King Xerxes. That was good news for Esther and her people, and it was destined to become a deadly surprise for Haman and his plans for promotion and power.

In the earliest days of the church, Israel's religious leaders in the Sanhedrin thought they were only dealing with some leftover renegade followers of a deceased renegade carpenter from Nazareth. In fact, they were actually threatening the chosen messengers of God and resisting His purposes. When they demanded that Peter and John no longer speak in the name of Jesus, they ceased to be merely the enemies of two disciples. They became the enemies of God.

That was good news for the disciples and bad news for the Sanhedrin. God answered the prayers of the disciples that day; signs and wonders became so prominent that thousands more believed the gospel of Christ and the church grew in spite of the persecution!

If your enemy is the King's enemy, then your battle is the King's battle. Are you doing the work and will of God in your life? If you encounter persecution, resistance, or open opposition while you pursue God's will God's way, then you don't have to worry about "winning the battle." Your battle has become God's battle. The King of kings himself is vitally interested in your success and well-being because you are interested in His kingdom and you pursue His presence. The Bible puts it this way: "If God is for us, who can be against us?"[1]

---

[1] Romans 8:31b.

PRAYER

Lord, I lean on You every day, and I seek first Your kingdom and Your righteousness. Consider the forces and circumstances arrayed against me. Consider their threats, hindrances, and opposition to Your purpose. My enemies have become Your enemies! If You are for me, who can be against me and still hope to succeed?

PERSONAL REFLECTIONS

Day Sixty-Six

DON'T UNDERESTIMATE THE POWER OF HOME-COURT ADVANTAGE!

The posture of "worship" is your home-court advantage.
Don't fight your personal Haman in the argumentative
mode; lure him into an atmosphere of worship!
Finding Favor With the King, 146

SCRIPTURE READING

ESTHER 5:4–5, WHERE ESTHER WISELY INVITED KING XERXES
AND HAMAN TO A BANQUET IN THE KING'S HONOR, AND
THE KING IMMEDIATELY ISSUED A ROYAL ORDER THAT
HAMAN BE PRESENT WHEN ESTHER PREPARED HER FEAST.

Home-court advantage is a very real force. It is so powerful and so coveted that collegiate and professional sports officials spend a great deal of time and resources jockeying for it. The favor present in "the home court" is so tangible that it can often mean the difference between a win and a loss!

Esther could not compete with the politically savvy schemes of Haman. Her enemy was a master conspirator with no scruples and an endless supply of hatred and envy fueling his evil designs. She wasn't a warrior, a captain of thousands, or even a business tycoon. But she did know what the king liked.

She shared an intimate relationship with the king that no royal title, military conquest, or political accomplishment could match. She effectively moved the battle from the royal court to the family dining room, where relationship always trumps formal protocol.

As I noted in *Finding Favor With the King,* "Most of us would have blurted out our request seconds after touching the king's scepter, and it is possible that in our haste we would have been denied. Satan often wants to divert us by convincing us to fight the *right battle* but on the *wrong battlefield*" (144).

Whatever "Haman" you face in life—whether it is financial crisis, disease, broken relationships, or persecution on behalf of Christ—don't fight against "flesh and blood." Put your problem on the altar of prayer, and begin to worship the King over your problem. This moves the battle out of the natural realm where your resources are almost certainly limited and very often ineffective.

Tap into the "home-court advantage" you enjoy when you enter the presence of the King as a son or daughter of God. The favor of God can tip the scales in virtually any situation when it is in line with God's Word and His eternal purposes.

Resist the urge to blurt out your petitions to Him the moment you enter His presence. It is your "right" under the rules of formal protocol, but the higher way is to worship Him, praise Him, and minister to Him as your first priority. Once the King is full and blessed through your banquet of adoration, you may whisper your request to Him as an intimate worshiper, knowing that He hears you and cares for you as His child.

This is where the power of home-court advantage kicks in, and this is the point where the enemy's plans get "kicked out" of the intimate atmosphere of worship.

===

PRAYER

Father, I'm preparing a rich banquet of praise, adoration, and worship for You in my heart. Will You meet me at the place of praise? And please invite my "Haman" to come along too—You know what I'm talking about.

PERSONAL REFLECTIONS

Day Sixty-Seven

PUT THE FIRST THING FIRST AND GET THE REST THROWN IN

Your first and most passionate petition
should be for the King's presence.
Finding Favor With the King, 147

═══

SCRIPTURE READING

ESTHER 5:6–8, WHERE ESTHER SET ASIDE HER PETITION
FOR THE DELIVERANCE OF THE JEWS FOR AN EVEN MORE
IMPORTANT PETITION: FOR THE PRESENCE OF THE
KING AND HER ENEMY AT A SECOND FEAST IN THE
KING'S HONOR.

═══

Jesus revealed the deeper truth behind Esther's secret when He said: "Seek first the kingdom of God and His righteousness, and all these things [money, clothing, food, and the basic essentials of life] shall be added to you."[1]

Esther had a life-and-death petition to deliver to King Xerxes. Her

---

[1]Matthew 6:33, bracketed mine.

first priority seemed obvious—surely the queen would skip the dinner party and get right down to business. After all, this was an important need!

It was true; Esther's petition was crucial. But the issue wasn't the importance of the petition. It was the importance and power of Esther's intimate relationship with the one who could extend favor. That relationship was more important than any gifts he could give to meet her needs.

Anyone who knew the basic protocols of the palace could present a petition to the king with a reasonable chance of getting what was asked for. Esther's situation as queen, and as the living "last hope" for her people, needed something more than protocol upon which to lean.

Are you the only follower of Christ in your family? Are you the lone intercessor standing in faith between eternity and your loved ones? Are you facing impossible challenges with a negative medical diagnosis or an impossible financial crisis? Are your children seemingly destroying themselves with bad choices and bad company? Is your local church struggling to survive against impossible odds?

You do have all of the rights of petition granted to those who know how to approach the throne in formal petition, framed and ordered in line with God's Word. We are commanded to come before the Lord on behalf of those in authority and make petition to the King. However, there are times when the privileges of intimate relationship will accomplish far more than formal petition. This was Esther's path.

Haman had as many rights of formal petition as she did. In fact, it appears that he controlled who had access and who was denied audience with the king—as long as they were formal affairs of the throne room. But he had no power to trump the queen's intimacy and privilege of family position. So Queen Esther moved the place of battle from the throne room to the dining room; she moved beyond the boundaries of formal protocol to the limitless realm of loving favor!

This is your privilege as well if you have given your heart and life to Jesus Christ and have become a child of God!

===

PRAYER

Father, our time together yesterday was wonderful, but I'm still hungry for more of Your presence today! Once again I've prepared a sumptuous feast of thanksgiving, praise, and lavish worship just for You. Only then, when You are well satisfied and blessed with my banquet of praise, will I whisper my desire in answer to Your waiting favor.

PERSONAL REFLECTIONS

Day Sixty-Eight

CORRECT
YOUR FOCUS PROBLEM

*Most of us have a genuine focus problem when it comes to
worship. We want to cling to our problems and the past
with one hand while offering God a miniature handful
of measured worship with the other.*
Finding Favor With the King, 150

SCRIPTURE READING

REVELATION 4:9–11, WHERE THE TWENTY-FOUR ELDERS
DESCRIBED BY THE APOSTLE JOHN OFFER CONTINUOUS,
EXTRAVAGANT, ALL-OUT, UNINHIBITED, AND LAVISH
WORSHIP AND PRAISE TO GOD.

Mommies and Daddies everywhere have experienced it: their little boys or girls carefully and extravagantly measure out one-half of one-third of a stick of chewing gum or a broken piece of cookie from their little hand and then climb into their laps to ask, "Daddy, Mommy, would you take me someplace and buy me a toy?"

It provokes a secret smile or chuckle when they are small, but when that same behavior continues into the teen years or, even worse, into adulthood, no one is smiling anymore.

Yet we do it to God nearly every week (and some of us may do it to Him several times a day!). We enter the Lord's presence with a mumbled "Thank You, Lord, for everything, I love You . . . now, about this problem of mine. You've really got to do something!"

In fact, the only measuring cup for worship in many of our churches bears the fictitious label, "Miniature, miserly measure of praise." Why? Perhaps it is because they want to rush past the "ooey, gooey stuff of relationship" to get to the divine promise and demanding petition part of their services. Our Father God is after the relationship. What are we there for?

Remember, it was Jesus who told us what matters most on God's shopping list: "But the hour is coming, and now is, when the true worshipers will worship the Father in spirit and truth; for the Father is seeking such to worship Him."[1]

John the apostle saw the twenty-four elders worshiping God continuously with lifted hands, with crowns cast down, and with their voices lifted in continuous praise, proclamations of honor, and worship. The closer we come to God and the greater we sense His manifest presence, the less worried we are about the lower concerns of earth. We begin to understand that in His presence, all things are made right. In His presence, His favor supplies our needs and much more besides. If we concern ourselves with satisfying our King, then He will concern himself with granting our petitions (sometimes even before they are spoken).

Avoid that faith-challenged habit of clinging more tightly to your grievances, needs, and petitions than to His hand. Great things happen when we approach God on bended knee, but the most important things happen when we whisper our desires from His lap while in the sweet communion of worship.

Are your problems filling "your hands" at the moment? Let go of your problems and your past long enough to give him "two hands worth" of wholehearted worship. When you return to those problems they will seem much smaller . . . if you can find them at all!

[1]John 4:23.

PRAYER

Father, excuse me while I lay down all of my concerns and worries. Please forgive me for being too preoccupied with those problems to focus on You. I want You more than I want any of those problems. I love You and I trust You for today and tomorrow.

PERSONAL REFLECTIONS

Day Sixty-Nine

LEARN TO WORSHIP WITH THE ENEMY AT YOUR TABLE!

Worship is never more important than when the enemy launches a plot to destroy your destiny!
Finding Favor With the King, 151

SCRIPTURE READING

ESTHER 6:13—7:6, WHEN HAMAN HAD BARELY RECOUNTED HIS BAD NEWS TO FAMILY AND FRIENDS BEFORE THE KING REQUIRED HIM TO SHOW UP FOR "PART TWO" OF ESTHER'S PRIVATE BANQUET OF HONOR. BY THE END OF *THAT* BANQUET, ESTHER'S ENEMY WOULD LEARN THAT HIS BAD TIMES WERE ABOUT TO GET INFINITELY WORSE, BECAUSE HE HAD BECOME THE KING'S ENEMY.

The ability to worship with the enemy at your table is a learned skill. Esther's first round of worship in the face of the enemy unleashed the favor of the king's heart. The second round released his swift judgment on her enemies.

By the second "round" or banquet of honor to King Xerxes, Esther's enemy was already wobbling and broken by the shifting tide of favor in his world.

Learn to worship God with the enemy at your table, and you will also discover the secret to delivering your family, your destiny, and perhaps even your nation from the plots and schemes of that enemy.

King David knew how to worship God even when he was literally surrounded by enemies:

"For in the time of trouble He shall hide me in His pavilion; in the secret place of His tabernacle He shall hide me; He shall set me high upon a rock. And now my head shall be lifted up above my enemies all around me; therefore I will offer sacrifices of joy in His tabernacle; I will sing, yes, I will sing praises to the Lord."[1]

He worshiped over his problems and kept his focus on the King, and in the end God elevated him to the place of king over Judah and Israel. Are you preparing your banquet for the King now?

It is one thing to see the enemy attack your reputation or bring persecution because of your devotion to the Lord. It is even more serious when he attempts to abort your destiny through an all-out attack. It is in those moments that worship becomes perhaps the most potent weapon in your spiritual arsenal when combined with God's unwavering Word.

Put those problems and the pressures of the enemy's onslaught at your feet and lift your eyes, your hands, and your hearts to the King. This is what I call "worshiping over your enemy." When Esther bypassed mere protocol to personally bless and honor the king, she moved the mighty Prime Minister Haman down to floor level while she ascended to the king's heart with her honoring ways.

Prepare a sacrifice of praise and call for a banquet tonight! Invite the Lord of Lords and King of Kings to a special banquet in His honor—and don't worry, your enemy will be there too.

---

[1] Psalm 27:5–6.

PRAYER

Lord, I've prepared a banquet just for You. It begins with a recounting of Your unmatched faithfulness topped with my deep gratitude and thankfulness. Then I will praise the wonder of Your love, Your kindness, and Your mercy; and finally, You will be given worship, honor, and the sacrifice of my lips and the offering of my body as a living sacrifice. I'm learning how to worship You no matter what circumstances may be camping out across from me at the time.

PERSONAL REFLECTIONS

Day Seventy

IGNORE THE ENEMY — WORSHIP THE KING!

If you learn to worship while the enemy sits across from you at the same table; if you can learn to pay such close attention to the King that you forget about the enemy staring you in the face . . . Then you win.

Finding Favor With the King, 153

SCRIPTURE READING

PSALM 37:4–5, WHERE WE ARE TOLD, "DELIGHT YOURSELF ALSO IN THE LORD, AND HE SHALL GIVE YOU THE DESIRES OF YOUR HEART. COMMIT YOUR WAY UNTO THE LORD, TRUST ALSO IN HIM, AND HE SHALL BRING IT TO PASS."

There is something about praise and worship offered in the face of impossible odds, crushing obstacles, and brokenhearted sorrow that honors God so greatly that He can't resist coming nearer.

He said it himself, but in these words, "The sacrifices of God are a broken spirit, a broken and a contrite heart; these, O God, you will not despise."[1]

---

[1] Psalm 51:17.

Have you ever watched a child facing a difficult sports challenge or an academic competition that seemed to be too great for him? I've noticed that some children manage to come out on top by keeping Mommy or Daddy in their vision somehow.

Every time they came up for air, or at each opportunity, their eyes searched the stands or audience for sight of Mom or Dad. All it took was a single "thumbs-up" sign, a grin, or a wink, and they were back in the competition with a vengeance!

In the depths of my vivid imagination, I can almost see the regal Queen Esther devoting her loving gaze exclusively to her husband and king, the mighty Xerxes. If I had been in Haman's place, I think I would have felt so uncomfortable and "unneeded" that I would have quietly excused myself from that intimate banquet meant for two.

You could be surrounded by sadness and encircled by crisis, but if you fill your view with God and His greatness, then you will be lifted to God's level as He draws you near to Him. As for the other unwanted and unneeded things . . . they should either remove themselves from your life or be prepared to *be* removed by the One you worship and adore.

You were created to praise and glorify God. Anything, any circumstance that attempts to limit or deny your ability to give Him glory, finds itself in the dangerous position of attempting to rob God.

When firemen come to the rescue of people trapped in burning buildings at dangerous heights, their first command as they move in on extension ladders, suspended from helicopters, or dangling from rescue lines, is simple: "Keep your eyes on me—and whatever you do, *don't look down.*"

The Lord would say the same thing to you. He is your "First Responder." He has heard your praise and is drawing near to your worship. But cooperate with Him—keep your eyes on Him. Whatever you do, *don't look down at your problems*! He will plant your feet on solid ground if you will only keep your focus on His face—even while your enemy grimaces in dismay!

PRAYER

Lord, I've set my hope on a sure thing—I'm banking my future and my destiny on Your faithfulness. No matter what happens, my eyes are upon You. I refuse to turn my eyes away to amplify my problems or measure my fears. I'm too busy taking in the height, the length, the breadth, and the depth of Your love!

PERSONAL REFLECTIONS

Day Seventy-One

WHAT ARE THE INGREDIENTS FOR A "THAT NIGHT"?

Have you ever needed a "that night"? Or a "that day"? An epoch-making event. A critical juncture. A crisis turning point. A point before which things were going wrong, but after which things began to go right? What are the ingredients for a "that night"?
Finding Favor With the King, 156

═══

SCRIPTURE READING

ESTHER 6:1 (KJV), WHERE WE READ, "ON *THAT NIGHT*, COULD NOT THE KING SLEEP" (EMPHASIS ADDED).

═══

S ome things seem to please God more than others. King Saul, for instance, discovered too late in his life that God *does* have a preference when presented the choice between our obedience or our sacrifice *to make up for our disobedience.*[1]

---

[1]See 1 Samuel 15:22, where Samuel the prophet rebuked Saul when he disobeyed God's direct command, and then tried to claim that he *had* obeyed.

The Bible says, "But without faith it is impossible to please Him, for he who comes to God must believe that He is, and that He is a rewarder of those who diligently seek Him."[2] Esther's bold decision to seek the king's face *before* she asked for favors or emergency actions from the power of his hands perfectly illustrates this Bible principle.

What are the components of a "that night" or a "that day" situation? Faith is the first component. And through faith comes the second all-important component—*relationship!*

It wasn't merely the good food and wine that captured King Xerxes' attention. This powerful Persian monarch didn't offer up to half of his kingdom to any of the cooks who actually prepared the food he and Haman enjoyed at those two banquets. As far as we know, he didn't offer so much as a weekend pass or kingly ball cap to the people who prepared and poured the wine, or set the table, or readied the dining room.

It seems that the people who actually did the *work* received nothing but the satisfaction of a job well done and the thankfulness of Queen Esther. The king directed all of the royal attention to *the one with the relationship*—the one who desired to bless and seek the face of the king. He was interested in hearing the heart's desire of that person, the one who had blessed his heart so well!

Are you in need of a "that night" to break free of depression and restore your dreams? Is your child or spouse in danger of falling for the enemy's schemes? Is that problem from your past, that crippling addiction that returns to trip you up again and again, seemingly impossible to defeat? If so, you are approaching a divinely appointed crisis turning point. The God who knows all things, who directs the steps of the righteous, has brought you to such a time and place as this. You are reading these words by divine design.

Could it be that if you will seek Him, trust Him, and surrender all to Him, then He will bring you to *"a point before which things were going wrong, but after which things begin to go right"*? He did it long ago in Persia for a woman named Esther. Why not now? Why not here? Why not *you?*

---

[2]Hebrews 11:6.

PRAYER

Father, You know the things I face that are just too big for me. I've exhausted my own limited strength, ideas, resources, and abilities. It is true—I'm in need of an "on that night" intervention from Your hand. But even more, I want You. I will seek Your face, even as I put all of my trust and faith in You, for You are faithful.

PERSONAL REFLECTIONS

Day Seventy-Two

ESTHER'S ULTIMATE SECRET REVEALED

Protocol of the Palace #8
Favor is what happens when preparation meets opportunity.
Finding Favor With the King, 157

≡

SCRIPTURE READING

MATTHEW 25:21, WHERE THE MASTER IN JESUS' PARABLE OF
THE TALENTS REWARDED HIS SERVANT, SAYING, "WELL
DONE, GOOD AND FAITHFUL SERVANT; YOU WERE FAITHFUL
OVER A FEW THINGS, I WILL MAKE YOU RULER OVER MANY
THINGS. ENTER INTO THE JOY OF YOUR LORD."

≡

I magine for a moment that your best friend had been born with the mental, neurological, and fine motor skills to be the world's greatest pianist or brain surgeon. That sounds exciting. Now picture that person spending most of his spare time in his teenage and college years sitting on a couch playing video games. (If this hits too close to home, I'm not sure I apologize.)

By the end of the "thirty-something" years, your friend has accumulated more loan default notices than exemplary grade reports. Somehow "destiny" has been missed, and regrets now dominate the "life-scape."

Was your imaginary friend's destiny a false hope? No. Was any "hard-wired equipment" missing? No. Only *one element* seems to be missing from this picture—*preparation.*

Talented and gifted young people from low-income, low-expectation families manage to rise above seemingly impossible odds to achieve their destinies despite their difficult environments. When one young person asked directions on how to get to Carnegie Hall, the response was practice, practice, practice!

Desire for their destiny seems to drive them in a desperate swim "upstream," and when preparation meets destiny—*favor* appears. As the Bible puts it, "A man's gift makes room for him, and brings him before great men."[1]

This is especially true in God's kingdom and in the lives of His children. God has *always* honored preparation and attention to detail, as long as it doesn't eclipse our central focus on worshiping and honoring Him.

"Esther was the ultimate *summa cum laude* graduate of the Chamberlain's School of Royal Protocol and Proper Preparation. She *knew* the great value of advance preparation" (156). First, she spent a full year preparing herself for one night with the king.

So when the crisis involving Haman's plot arose, she knew exactly how to prepare herself physically and spiritually (through corporate prayer and fasting) for a meeting with her *destiny.*

"Go, gather all the Jews who are present in Shushan, and fast for me; neither eat nor drink for three days, night or day. My maids and I will fast likewise. And so I will go to the king, which *is* against the law; and if I perish, I perish!"[2]

Queen Esther *counted* on God's favor showing up to bring deliverance to her, her family, and her people. Protocol alone couldn't save her. This was a job for divine favor and the intervention of God.

---

[1]Proverbs 18:16.
[2]Esther 4:16.

Are you in a life situation that mere protocol cannot touch? Remember your destiny and make the necessary preparations to take your desire to the King of Kings. Favor will meet you there—in His presence!

═══

PRAYER

Father, it's me again. I love to be with You and sense Your presence in my life. No one comforts me, encourages me, or strengthens me like You do. I feel as if I'm surrounded by negative reports and contrary circumstances, but I'm preparing my best gift in my heart right now—and it is just for You.

PERSONAL REFLECTIONS

Day Seventy-Three

INDULGENT WORSHIP
CREATES A
SLEEPLESS KING

*Do you understand that the King of Kings and Lord of
Lords can't say no to you? That is, if you are His bride,
clothed in praise and arrayed in righteousness! He said,
"Ask, and it shall be given."[1] God finds it hard to say no to
you. In fact, He can't if you ask "according to His will."[2]*
Finding Favor With the King, 159

═══

SCRIPTURE READING

DANIEL 10:12 (NASB), WHERE THE ANGEL OF THE LORD
SPOKE MANY THINGS TO DANIEL, INCLUDING THIS
AMAZING STATEMENT: *"YOUR WORDS WERE HEARD*, AND I
HAVE COME *IN RESPONSE TO YOUR WORDS."*

═══

B y this point in the history of Esther's life in ancient Persia, it is
clear that "God's powerful behind-the-scenes intervention in

---

[1]Matthew 7:7 KJV.
[2]See 1 John 5:14–15.

human affairs is evident in the sleepless night of King Xerxes" (157). We know from the Scriptures that the Almighty *never* sleeps or slumbers,[3] but He often causes men and women to awaken from sound sleep or prevents them from sleeping until His purposes are prepared or accomplished for the next day. And many times His work in the night hours or hidden places is released *in response to* our prayers, praise, and worship. To think otherwise is to void the power of prayer altogether.

Daniel prayed and sought God's face daily on behalf of his people, and an angel of the Lord pulled aside the veil to reveal the inner workings of prayer and God's response in the heavenly realm.

In Daniel's case, the angel made it clear that God *heard Daniel's prayer and answered it* the very day it was offered up: "From the first day that you set your heart on understanding this and on humbling yourself before your God, *your words were heard*, and I have come *in response to your words*."[4] The arrival of God's answer, however, was delayed (but not stopped) for twenty-one days by demonic interference in the heavenlies.

The final book of the Bible reinforces the truth that God hears our prayers and stores up our praise, and that He *acts* on them in His time. The Bible says the twenty-four elders fall down before God's throne with "golden bowls full of incense, *which are the prayers of the saints*."[5]

And finally, the principles we see in Esther's life and the outright statement by James the apostle: "The effective, fervent prayer of a righteous man avails much"[6] make it clear that God honors prayer from someone who is *righteous*, someone who prays effectively and with passion.

Have you *prayed* about the difficult or challenging situations in your life? Make sure you've taken care of any wrong motives, unforgiveness, or unconfessed sin in your life. Then prepare a banquet for the Lord through a genuine outpouring of your love in the form of thanksgiving, praise, worship, adoration, and a lifestyle that says yes to Him in word and deed.

---

[3]See Psalm 121:3–4.
[4]Daniel 10:12b NASB.
[5]Revelation 5:8b.
[6]James 5:16b.

This is how you make sure you pray His will instead of merely your wants while also seeking His face as your First Love rather than merely your First Source.

<hr>

PRAYER

Father, I know You value honesty and expect no less than total honesty from me when I seek You. So I admit to You that it seems hard to believe that you find it hard to say no to me at any time. But Your Word is my anchor, not merely my opinion. I seek You and Your kingdom first. Thank You for supplying my needs and the needs of those I love. I know that You hear me, and that you reward those who diligently seek You. Because I continually say yes to You and Your will, I am assured by Your Word that You say yes to me as well.

PERSONAL REFLECTIONS

Day Seventy-Four

FEELING THE EFFECTS OF DIVINE INSOMNIA

Jesus often spent sleepless nights during His earthly stay as He prayed over impending challenges facing those He loved. Perhaps our heavenly King still paces the golden floors of Heaven—not in paranoid fear but in passionate love— feeling the effects of divine insomnia.
Finding Favor With the King, 160–61

═══

SCRIPTURE READING

LUKE 22:31–32 (KJV), WHERE JESUS WARNED PETER
THAT SATAN DESIRED TO SIFT HIM AS WHEAT,
AND IN THE SAME BREATH TOLD HIM,
"BUT I HAVE PRAYED FOR THEE,
THAT THY FAITH FAIL NOT:
AND WHEN THOU ART CONVERTED,
STRENGTHEN THY BRETHREN"
(ITALICS MINE).

═══

I t seems our God really does not sleep, nor does He need or require sleep if my understanding of the Scriptures is correct. However, there are certain issues or situations that seem to move the Lord to *do something on our behalf.*[1]

The apostle John allows us to eavesdrop on the Lord's prayer for His disciples then and now: "*I pray for them.* I do not pray for the world but for those whom You have given Me, for they are Yours. . . . I do not pray that You should take them out of the world, but that You should *keep them from the evil one.*"[2]

The Lord's prayers for His followers didn't stop with that prayer offered in His final days, nor did they stop when He gave His life on the cross and later ascended to heaven. Do you realize that your King, the Lord of Lords, prays for you day and night—especially when you seek Him first and make your life conform to His will?

How do we know this? He tells us in His Word: "Therefore He [Jesus Christ] is also able to save to the uttermost those who come to God through Him, since He always lives to make intercession for them."[3]

In another place, the Bible says, "It is Christ who died, and furthermore is also risen, who is even at the right hand of God, who also makes intercession for us."[4] Not only does God sometimes cause human beings to lose sleep until His purposes are accomplished, but He also is tirelessly interceding and praying on our behalf as well!

Although the human King Xerxes bore little resemblance in character or in anointing to Jesus Christ, his sleepless night on righteous Mordecai's behalf is a picture of the way our great King forsakes sleep to intercede for our safety and the fulfillment of His purposes in our lives. No matter what you face at the moment, if you have submitted yourself to God, then this promise is for you:

"Therefore submit to God. Resist the devil and he will flee from you. Draw near to God and He will draw near to you. . . . Humble yourselves in the sight of the Lord, and He will lift you up."[5]

---

[1] I am firmly convinced from the Scriptures that we are forgiven and saved by faith alone, faith in Christ Jesus and His complete redemptive work on the cross. But I am also convinced that He prays for us day and night, even at this moment.
[2] John 17:9, 15, italics mine.
[3] Hebrews 7:25, italics mine.
[4] Romans 8:34b, italics mine.
[5] James 4:7–8a, 10.

PRAYER

Father, I submit myself to You. I resist the devil, knowing he must flee from me according to Your Word. I'm drawing close to You, humbling myself in Your sight. Lord Jesus, it reassures me to know that you live forever and You are praying for me day and night. I trust You, Lord, knowing that You will lift me up in due season.

PERSONAL REFLECTIONS

Day Seventy-Five

WHAT DOES GOD EAT WHEN HE IS REALLY HUNGRY?

Twelve professional preachers went into that village [Sychar in Samaria], and all they brought Jesus was a Happy Meal; one transformed worshiper ran into that village, and the Bible says she brought "many of the Samaritans of that city" to Jesus!
Finding Favor With the King, 163–64

———

SCRIPTURE READING

JOHN 4:5–34, WHERE JESUS ENCOUNTERED "THE WOMAN AT THE WELL" IN SAMARIA, AND "FEASTED" ON THE WORSHIP AND HUNGER FOR GOD'S PRESENCE THAT HE FOUND IN THAT REJECTED AND DOWNTRODDEN WOMAN.

———

The Samaritan woman responded with childlike exuberance once she understood what Jesus was revealing to her. After spending only a matter of minutes in the presence of Jesus, her immediate response was to *run* back home and tell others about the wonderful man she had just met.

Keep in mind that Jesus said, "Assuredly, I say to you, whoever does not receive the kingdom of God as a little child will by no means enter it."[1]

The disciples, on the other hand, who had spent a considerable amount of time with Jesus, were buying food at that same village, but they didn't seem to feel it important to share the good news about the special guest resting at Jacob's well. (Given the racial and religious animosity between Jews and Samaritans, perhaps the disciples felt Samaritans weren't "worth" the effort.)

The disciples were surprised when Jesus refused the food that they brought back from town, so the Lord took that opportunity to teach them about His true "meat," the sustaining food for His life. "My food is to do the will of Him who sent me, and to finish His work."[2] That "work" was to preach the gospel of the kingdom to *everyone* who wanted to walk with God. That even included Samaritans, the despised "mixed Jews" who were traditionally treated as "unclean" by the Jews of Jesus' day.

Jesus told the Samaritan woman that the heavenly Father seeks worshipers who will worship Him in spirit and truth.[3] I can't help but ask, *"Shouldn't we be seeking out such worshipers too?"*

Isn't that what happens when we share the gospel with others and see them receive Christ and enter God's kingdom? *This is how we do our part to increase the level of worship and the number of worshipers in the kingdom.*

The disciples still didn't understand that the good news of the kingdom was as much for the people "outside the church" as it was for those who were already on the inside—a problem we still seem to struggle with today.

How about you?

---

[1] Mark 10:15.
[2] John 4:34b.
[3] See John 4:23.

Do you tend to be more excited about lunch after church than about skipping lunch to reach your friends with the good news about the One who changed your life so dramatically?

≡

PRAYER

Father, I know we are all *called to preach the good news to the lost, but even more than being a "professional preacher," I want to be a* transformed worshiper *who boldly tells others about Your love. Lord Jesus, may my love for You and my astonishment over Your selfless act on the cross only grow stronger with each new day!*

PERSONAL REFLECTIONS

Day Seventy-Six

WHEN WORSHIP PRODUCES THE "THUNDERINGS OF DIVINE UNREST"

When we set a banqueting table for our King that spills over with adoration, love, and the sweet fragrance of worship and praise, we "stuff" Him with our abundant worship. Then, "that night" the King of Kings arises from His throne in holy restlessness. He who never slumbers begins to shake the heavens with thunderings of divine unrest.

Finding Favor With the King, 164

≡

SCRIPTURE READING

ACTS 4:5–31, WHERE THE APOSTLES REACTED TO THEIR FIRST EXPERIENCE OF PERSECUTION AFTER THE RESURRECTION WITH CORPORATE PRAISE AND WORSHIP TO GOD, A RECOUNTING OF HIS PROPHECIES, AND A REQUEST FOR GREATER BOLDNESS WITH SIGNS AND WONDERS FOLLOWING. AND GOD ANSWERED THEM *BY SHAKING THE BUILDING THEY WERE IN* AND BY *FILLING THEM AFRESH WITH THE HOLY SPIRIT AND BOLDNESS.*

T hose who believe God is a retired and disinterested Caretaker of an essentially abandoned creation will have trouble with this one, but perhaps they should read the Bible. It is clear from the Scriptures that God *does* answer prayer and that He *responds to spiritual hunger in the human heart*!

In the story of the Samaritan woman at the well, the supposed "end" of the story marks the beginning of another even more intriguing tale! The newly transformed woman ran to her village and brought a crowd of her neighbors back to meet Jesus—and something unusual happened:

"In fact, this is one of those rare instances where *visitation turned into habitation,* because He ended up staying three more days ministering to this non-Jewish town!

"It's obvious this village had favor from Jesus. He extended the revival! They met His worship need!" (164).

God can't pass up the call of a broken and contrite heart. Nor will He ignore the adoration and praise of true worshipers. Even His mighty judgments in the book of Revelation are released with heavenly thunderings, lightnings, and an earthquake only *after* the prayers of the saints are mixed with incense and released as sweet fragrance to God.[1]

In the book of Acts, immediately after Peter and John were seized and threatened by the high priests and the Sanhedrin, they met with other believers and began to recount God's mighty acts and glory. Then the disciples asked God to act on their behalf so they could proclaim the gospel boldly. The answer they received was nothing less than miraculous:

"And when they had prayed, the place where they were assembled together was shaken; and they were all filled with the Holy Spirit, and they spoke the word of God with boldness."[2]

---

[1]See Revelation 8:3–6.
[2]Acts 4:31.

God responds to corporate praise and worship, especially when it is offered by people who are of one mind and one soul. In this case, God's response marked the thunderings of divine unrest *and* the thunderings of divinity blessed!

═══

PRAYER

Father, it comforts me to know that You care. It reassures me to know that You are able to shake heaven and hell on my behalf if necessary. I will praise You and worship You in the congregation. I will offer You sweet fragrances of thanksgiving, praise, worship, adoration, awe, fear, and joy unspeakable. I welcome Your shaking, lightning, and thunderings as long as I can draw near to You and bear good fruit that pleases You.

PERSONAL REFLECTIONS

Day Seventy-Seven

NEVER UNDERESTIMATE THE POWER OF FAVOR

The enemies of God and of the people of His purpose should never forget—it is dangerous to attack those who have favor with the King. Haman was about to experience the unmatched pain of God's justice: a complete reversal of fortunes in the time it takes for the king to utter one fateful command.
Finding Favor With the King, 169

SCRIPTURE READING

ESTHER 6:4–12, WHERE GOD TURNS THE TABLES ON HAMAN'S SCHEMES *AFTER* THE SLEEPLESS KING XERXES IS COMPELLED TO "CHECK THE RECORDS" AND DISCOVERS MORDECAI'S UNREWARDED DEED.

Favor often seems to work unseen, behind the scenes and silently in the realm of the human heart, thought processes, and emotions. An employer suddenly senses that he should grant a raise to a particular employee and really doesn't understand why. On "impulse," a car dealer decides to drop the price another $1,100 for a Christian couple while secretly wondering, "What's wrong with me?"

Neither Esther nor Mordecai realized that God's favor was at work on "that night." In fact, everything *appeared* to be going Haman's way!

"Perhaps, unknown to you, a divine reversal has begun in the court of heaven. Take this lesson from Esther: *Never underestimate the power of favor*" (169).

If we are honest with one another, most of us will admit that we are continually *surprised* by God's faithfulness and favor in our lives. Perhaps that is because we habitually underestimate the *power* of favor, and God's willingness to grant heavenly favor to people on earth.

In Esther's day, and for centuries afterward, a king's favor was the most powerful earthly force available on earth. A king's favor could actually cover and pardon a convicted criminal from all criminal charges and punishments. It could countermand the rulings of the highest court, and set aside the most ancient of laws.

The king's favor simultaneously deals a death blow to the evil designs of enemies while distributing blessings and abundant provision to those the king wishes to honor.

Are you facing an impossible situation right now? Do you feel unjust persecution and false accusation have positioned you for misunderstanding, separation, or outright persecution?

"Most of us will encounter difficult days or overwhelming crises when we need a 'that night.' Not just any day will do; we need a 'that night' or a 'that day' to set in motion the intervening favor of a King who never forgets" (169).

Our heavenly King really *doesn't forget* the good things we've done, and He actually says so in His Word: "For God is not unjust to forget your work and labor of love which you have shown toward His name, in that you have ministered to the saints, and do minister."[1]

Will you set your eyes and your faith upon Him? Believe God, and *never underestimate the power of favor*!

---

[1]Hebrews 6:10.

≡

PRAYER

Father, You know what I face each day. You also know about my failures and fears—even though I sometimes try to hide them. Many times in the past, I actually underestimated the power of Your favor in my life, and I feel I missed out because of it. But today is a new day, with new hope and new faith.

I thank You that divine favor is at work on my behalf at this very moment, moving and shifting resources, obstacles, and even the hearts of people. Thank You.

PERSONAL REFLECTIONS

Day Seventy-Eight

WHEN HALFWAY WON'T DO, TIMING IS EVERYTHING

Why [did Queen Esther] continue to turn down an offer for up to "half the kingdom"? Who wouldn't want half of the Persian empire? Perhaps someone with a death sentence hanging over her head, someone who sees a dark cloud of ethnic cleansing drawing closer and closer to her people— half measures and half kingdoms simply wouldn't do.

Finding Favor With the King, 172

———

SCRIPTURE READING

GALATIANS 4:4–5 (KJV), WHERE WE SEE THAT
GOD HIMSELF *WAITED* UNTIL
"THE FULNESS OF THE TIME WAS COME"
BEFORE HE SENT HIS SON,
HIS COMPLETE SOLUTION FOR A FALLEN WORLD,
"TO REDEEM THEM THAT WERE UNDER THE LAW,
THAT WE MIGHT RECEIVE THE ADOPTION OF SONS."

═══

People who are content with halfway measures, cheap favors, or quick pleasures rarely worry about timing. They want what they want fast, easy, and trouble-free. Much of the time these three phrases describe the very *opposite* of God's perfect will for us and for His kingdom on earth. It is nearly impossible to bypass quick fixes and easy solutions to wait for God's "best" unless you are led by the Spirit of God.

"For as many as are led by the Spirit of God, these are sons of God. For you did not receive the spirit of bondage again to fear, but you received the Spirit of adoption by whom we cry out, "Abba, Father.""[1]

With all of the pressure bearing down on Queen Esther during the first and second banquets—with a death sentence over her head and with her enemy leering at her from across their intimate dinner setting with the king—no one would have held it against her had she taken the king's offer of "up to half of the kingdom" and blurted out her petition. No one, that is, except God, who had carefully prepared a *divine solution* to an essentially *spiritual* problem.

Esther might have managed to overturn Haman's death orders for the Jews, but *she didn't even know about the plot to murder Mordecai.* And through it all, King Xerxes probably would have entertained serious doubts about the guilt of his prime minister.[2] God had a better idea that would take care of every problem perfectly and permanently, but it would only come to pass if Esther held out through two rounds of "good offers" for God's "very best."

Are you facing serious problems but sense that God might have a better way to do things? Do you fear you can't handle "the wait" it may require or "the weight" of the pressure it is likely to place on your faith?

Don't run from the wait or the weight that comes with a commit-

---

[1] Romans 8:14–15.
[2] See Esther 3:8–15.

ment to seek God's face. He will give you the strength to stand, the patience to persevere, and the reward to justify every sacrifice you make! Seek the King's face, not His hand.

===

PRAYER

Father, I'm not sure I can handle the pressures of delay or faithful waiting. I am really tempted to take halfway solutions and easy answers and then run, but I know better because I've come to know You. I cast my cares upon You because I know You care for me.[3] I've made up my mind and settled it in my heart: As for me and my house, we will serve the Lord.[4]

PERSONAL REFLECTIONS

[3]See 1 Peter 5:7.
[4]See Joshua 24:15b.

Day Seventy-Nine

I OPENED MY MOUTH TO SAY "NO" AND "YES" CAME OUT!

Esther desperately needed the help of Xerxes to save the lives of all the Jews under the control of the Persian empire, but she knew the danger of asking the right question *at the* wrong time. *Wisdom is learning the right time to ask the right question.*

Finding Favor With the King, 177

═══

SCRIPTURE READING

SECOND SAMUEL 6, WHERE DAVID "ASKED THE SAME QUESTION" TWICE WITH *DIFFERENT RESULTS* WHEN BRINGING THE ARK OF THE COVENANT TO JERUSALEM.

═══

Extravagant demonstrations of devotion do funny things to people—and they even touch the heart of God. Yet extravagance and devotion alone aren't enough. Obedience and careful observance of God's desires and timing can make all the difference between divine blessings and disaster (which is often produced by "presumption" in the mix).

King David wanted to bring the ark of the covenant (where God's *shekinah* presence dwelt in those days) to Jerusalem. He assembled a parade of thousands to do the deed, but his first attempt produced death and disappointment. He had plenty of extravagant worship and devotion, but it was mixed with presumption. The second time around, David carefully avoided presumption and followed God's protocol of intimacy *plus* obedience, and successfully brought the ark of God's glory to Jerusalem.

The Roman centurion who appealed to Jesus exhibited such faith that the Lord praised him *above everyone else*—Jew or Gentile—that He had ever met! For much of the Lord's ministry, He had concentrated on reaching the Jewish people. It is possible that the faith of this non-Jewish Roman soldier *moved and amazed* the Savior so much that it turned His "no" into a "yes" to the man's request.[1]

The Syro-Phoenician woman who persisted in her request on behalf of her demon-possessed daughter *literally* turned a divine "no" into a divine "yes"!

"The woman was a Greek, a Syro-Phoenician by birth, and she kept asking Him to cast the demon out of her daughter. But Jesus said to her, 'Let the children be filled first, for it is not good to take the children's bread and throw it to the little dogs.' And she answered and said to Him, 'Yes, Lord, yet even the little dogs under the table eat from the children's crumbs.' Then He said to her, *'For this saying* go your way; the demon has gone out of your daughter.' "[2]

God doesn't "change His mind," but He does often wait until we catch up to and align our thinking with His. The woman was persistent because somehow she had grasped and understood the nature of God. She knew that the Lord could and *would* heal her daughter, so she persevered through every test and obstacle based on that *belief.* Her unwavering faith unlocked the door in the Lord's heart and seemingly caused Him to open His mouth to say "no" and "yes" came out!

[1]See Matthew 8:5–13.
[2]Mark 7:26–29, emphasis mine.

═══

PRAYER

Father, despite what I see and feel at the moment, I trust You, and I am expecting the best to come my way because I've humbled myself before You—and I'm staying.

PERSONAL REFLECTIONS

Day Eighty

PETITION FROM THE POSITION OF INTIMATE RELATIONSHIP

Esther teaches us there is an even better way: Learn how to enter the King's presence and petition from the position of intimate relationship.
Finding Favor With the King, 178

===

SCRIPTURE READING

FIRST KINGS 1:15–31, WHERE BATHSHEBA INTERCEDED WITH HER HUSBAND, KING DAVID, FOR HER LIFE AND THE LIFE OF HER FAMILY AT THE ADVICE OF HER VERY OWN "MORDECAI," THE PROPHET NATHAN. DAVID WAS NEAR DEATH, BUT HE RESPONDED TO THE PLEAS HIS WIFE OFFERED "FROM THE POSITION OF INTIMATE RELATIONSHIP." HE OVERRULED THE PRESUMPTUOUS CLAIM OF ANOTHER SON TO THE THRONE THAT WAS BASED ON LEGAL SUPPOSITION, AND INSTALLED SOLOMON—HIS SON BY BATHSHEBA—AS HIS LEGAL SUCCESSOR.

If you look closely at the prayers you offer to God, you may notice that sometimes you petition or make requests to the King of Kings based on formal protocol and "legal argument" from the Scriptures.

To a certain extent, this is proper and good. However, everything goes wrong when we allow presumption, wrong motives, or selfishness to contaminate and infiltrate our petitions to the Lord. I even describe in *Finding Favor With the King* how these things show up in church services from time to time:

"Sometimes we rush into church and push through our planned religious activities so we can throw our requests at God like ungrateful children, pawing for His hands and digging through His infinite pockets for private treasure" (178).

In fact, we are *commanded* to make certain "prayer petitions" in the New Testament:

"First of all, then, I urge that *entreaties* and prayers, *petitions* and thanksgivings, be made on behalf of all men, for kings and all who are in authority, so that we may lead a tranquil and quiet life in all godliness and dignity."[1]

The most effective prayers—those of a much more intimate and passionate form—are used when praying on behalf of those we know and with whom we share a covenant bond.

James the apostle said, "Confess your faults one to another, and *pray one for another*, that ye may be healed. The effectual fervent prayer of a righteous man availeth much."[2]

However, the *most effective prayers* offered to God are based on our "sonship" or the intimate family relationship with Him that we receive through Christ Jesus. This is the central key to offering petitions *from*

---

[1] 1 Timothy 2:1 NASB, emphasis mine.
[2] James 5:16 KJV, emphasis mine.

the position of intimate relationship: "And because you are sons, God has sent forth the Spirit of His Son into your hearts, crying out, 'Abba, Father!' Therefore you are no longer a slave but a son, and if a son, then an heir of God through Christ."[3]

Assume you have an enemy who hates you without reason and is totally dedicated to your humiliation, degradation, and ultimate destruction. (By the way, you *do* have an enemy like that named Satan).

Now, would you rather stand before God's throne and present your petition for help based on your need (mere need doesn't seem to move God), or move close to His side and whisper your request to Him as His son or daughter? The answer seems obvious, doesn't it?

═══

PRAYER

Father, You already know about the needs in my life and You know about the fears I sometimes carry around in my mind. I surrender my fears to You, and I come to You with a heart filled with praise to cry out, "Abba, Daddy, Father!" As for my needs—I want to praise and worship You some more. Then, I may ask You something. . . .

PERSONAL REFLECTIONS

---

[3]Galatians 4:6–7, emphasis mine.

Day Eighty-One

YOU'VE WON MY HEART ... WHICH HALF OF MY KINGDOM DO YOU WANT?

I turned to my daughter and said, "Come on baby,
let's go." We drove into town and pulled up in front
of a toy store. Keep in mind that my daughter hadn't asked
for anything, but by the time she finished loving on me,
I wanted to walk in the toy store and say right out loud,
"Which half of the store do you want?
This half or that half?"
Finding Favor With the King, 181

———

SCRIPTURE READING

ESTHER 5:3, 6; 7:2, PASSAGES THAT RECORD THE
THREE TIMES KING XERXES OFFERED TO GRANT
THE REQUEST AND PETITION OF QUEEN ESTHER,
"UP TO HALF OF THE KINGDOM."

G od is not a "respecter of persons" when it comes to favoring one of His obedient children over another.[1] *However,* He absolutely does "show favorites" when it comes to blessing, protecting, and favoring His children who live among those who do not serve God or acknowledge Him. And He always has been and always will be "a rewarder of those who diligently seek Him."[2]

In real estate, the driving phrase for maximum value and return on investment is "Location, location, location." In God's kingdom, the driving phrase for maximum blessing and giving God glory is "Attitude, attitude, attitude."

God will not bless a proud spirit, selfish motives, or a lawless and rebellious heart. But He delights in heart-felt praise, genuine repentance, and all-out worship.

In the story about my daughter's "wooing" skills as a six-year-old, I knew all along that even though my daughter *did* love me and did want to shower me with displays of a little girl's affection, she *also* would enjoy a gift or blessing from my hand. What "undid" me and melted my heart was her persistent determination to set aside her requests and wants just to bless her daddy.

There is abundant evidence in the Bible that God is even *more* responsive to genuine displays of love from His people. He actually spoke prophetically through Isaiah saying:

"For thus says the High and Lofty One who inhabits eternity, whose name is Holy: 'I dwell in the high and holy place, with him who has a contrite and humble spirit, to revive the spirit of the humble, and to revive the heart of the contrite ones.'"[3]

[1]We know this because God says so in His Word (see Acts 10:34–35, where the apostle Peter declares essentially the same thing you just read in the pages of this book).
[2]See Hebrews 11:6.
[3]Isaiah 57:15, emphasis mine.

Elsewhere, David declared: "But thou art holy, *O thou that inhabitest the praises* of Israel."[4]

So God inhabits eternity *with* those having contrite and humble spirits. And He *literally* inhabits our praises! (Some translations say He is "enthroned" upon or in our praises!)

The next time you go to the Lord, hold back your request list long enough to build a throne for Him with your praises. Sing His praises, offer your thanksgivings in lavish detail, and whisper to Him how much you love Him simply because *He is.*

Then when He is full and satisfied with the bounty of praise, worship, and adoration you have prepared, He just might whisper back to you, "Now tell me your request; what can I do for you, My beloved child?"

PRAYER

Father, thank You for your faithfulness and for the love You pour over me every day. I love You and hunger for Your presence. Teach me how to please You—for You have surely blessed me. I have a request, but first, I just want to praise You more. . . .

PERSONAL REFLECTIONS

---

[4]Psalm 22:3 KJV, emphasis mine.

Day Eighty-Two

WHEN THE KING "WORKS THE NIGHT SHIFT WITH YOU IN MIND"

"Let me serve you first in another feast of abundance.
Then *I will tell you my heart's desire." It is at this point*
of incredible anticipation that Esther leaves Xerxes so
stuffed with the abundance of her banquet, so enamored
by her beauty, and so eager to hear her request
that he cannot sleep.
Finding Favor With the King, 182

═══

SCRIPTURE READING

PSALM 42:1–9, WHERE WE SEE A WORD PORTRAIT OF TRUE
PASSION FOR GOD'S INTIMATE PRESENCE THAT WAS
REVEALED THOUSANDS OF YEARS AGO—BEGINNING IN THE
LIFE AND REIGN OF DAVID, THE SWEET PSALMIST OF
ISRAEL, AND PERFECTLY CAPTURED BY WORSHIP SINGERS
CALLED "THE SONS OF KORAH."

God tells us in His Word that He is drawn and attracted to certain things. He promises to *respond* whenever and wherever He finds these things in abundance. He is attracted to repentant or contrite hearts, and from the beginning, it has been His habit to meet with those who seek Him.[1]

Jesus said His Father so desires those who will worship Him "in spirit and truth" that He personally seeks them out in the earth![2] Think about that. God Almighty, the creator of heaven and earth, leaves His celestial throne to seek *you* out and enjoy your unique gift prepared just for Him!

The Christian life is not a *spectator sport*. To be a Christian is to love God fervently, passionately, *all the time*. Both the Old and New Testaments tell us in no uncertain terms that the first and greatest commandment of God is "Thou shalt love the Lord thy God with all thy heart, and with all thy soul, and with all thy mind."[3]

Jesus said, "Seek [pursue, desire, endeavor to acquire] first the kingdom of God and His righteousness."[4]

Jesus did *not* say, "Try to *like* God's kingdom . . . hang out there awhile . . . enjoy the nuance of the atmosphere . . . get all the goosebump religion you can before you leave the building and *live the same way you lived before you came.*"

When you worship Him first, and seek to bless Him more than you seek His blessings, something wonderful happens in the heart of God. It must be somewhat like the condition in which King Xerxes found himself after Queen Esther's banquet, sleepless and "stuffed with abundance,

---

[1]See Psalm 34:18; 51:17; 63:1; Proverbs 8:17; Isaiah 55:6; 57:15; 66:2; and 2 Chronicles 15:2.
[2]See John 4:23–24.
[3]Jesus quoted this to a Jewish lawyer in Matthew 22:37 KJV, and it also appears in Deuteronomy 6:5; 11:1; 19:9; 30:6; 30:20; Mark 12:30; and Luke 10:27.
[4]Matthew 6:33, insertion in brackets mine.

enamored by beauty, and ready to hear."[5]

We don't "buy" or "earn" God's special favor, but He *is* a *rewarder* of those who diligently seek Him![6] He *does* treasure our praises, and He stores up our prayers and worship! It doesn't take much brainpower to figure out what blesses God at this point.

When we put the Lord's desires above our own, and seek to please Him more than ourselves, He *responds*! We cannot out-give or out-love God—it is an eternal impossibility—but I suspect He loves it when we try! As we noted in *Finding Favor With the King:* "When the King 'works the night shift with you in mind,' destinies are raised from the ashes of evil plots, and high strategies of destruction against good people are struck down" (182).

━━━━

PRAYER

Father, I will seek You early and I will seek You in the evening hours. You are my chief delight, my Rock, and my Fortress. Blessed be Your name forever. I put my trust in You, my satisfaction and joy. You already know the sum of my needs and I commit them to You.

PERSONAL REFLECTIONS

---

[5]Adapted from *Finding Favor With the King,* 182.
[6]See Hebrews 11:6, as we noted in an earlier devotional.

Day Eighty-Three

REFINE YOUR PURSUIT

This leads us to what may be one of the greatest of all the lessons in Esther's life: Refine your pursuit to the point where you genuinely value the King more than the kingdom; you'll be amazed to discover what the King will do for you.
Finding Favor With the King, 183–84

≡

SCRIPTURE READING

FIRST CHRONICLES 17, IN WHICH KING DAVID SAT IN HIS HOUSE *THINKING ABOUT HOW TO BUILD A HOUSE FOR GOD.* BEFORE THE CHAPTER ENDS, GOD PROMISES TO "BUILD A HOUSE" FOR DAVID THAT WOULD NEVER END, PROPHESYING THE COMING OF THE MESSIAH FROM DAVID'S FAMILY LINE.

≡

S ome people seem to forget about God once the blessings start flowing their direction. They forget about prayer because their golf dates, business deals, shopping trips, and home-building plans seem to take over their schedules. They have no problem making God their "go-to God" when things go wrong, but they have a "devil of a problem" serving God when everything is going right.

David seemed to avoid that problem for most of his life. His habit of focusing on God seemed to have begun in his early years of tending sheep, but we find him thinking about God's welfare and happiness often in the Scriptures. David sat in a "house of cedar" thinking about God. He just couldn't bear the thought of living in a nice home while God resided in the ark of the covenant under a mere tent. He "refined his pursuit" to value God more than His blessings and unleashed the bountiful giving heart of God on his family and on the world.

The Lord described the blessings He had already given David, and then He started adding *more*, beginning with these promises: "Also I will subdue all your enemies. Furthermore I tell you that the Lord will build you a house."[1] The next chapter describes all of the enemies David defeated one by one. By the time his son, Solomon, assumed the throne, all of Israel's enemies had been defeated!

Queen Esther had refined her pursuit to look after the desires of King Xerxes more than her own, and through the favor it produced, she saved her own life and the lives of her people. She also saw Mordecai promoted to Haman's position of power under the king!

Jesus said, "When you pray, do not use vain repetitions as the heathen do. For they think that they will be heard for their many words. Therefore do not be like them. *For your Father knows the things you have need of before you ask Him.*"[2]

If your Father knows what you need even before you ask Him, doesn't it make even *more* sense to focus on Him rather than on your needs? Refine your pursuit! Genuinely value the Lord more than anything He can give you or do for you . . . and you will be amazed to discover what He will do for you!

---

[1] 1 Chronicles 17:10b.
[2] Matthew 6:7–8, emphasis mine.

—————

PRAYER

Father, I'm moving aside all of my requests, complaints, hurts, and needs because I have something much more important to bring to You right now—my mouth is filled with praise, my thoughts overflow with gratitude and thanksgiving to You, and my heart is bursting with love, desire, and adoration for You!

PERSONAL REFLECTIONS

Day Eighty-Four

ENTERING THE PLACE OF WORSHIP AND INTIMACY

If you can forget about your needs long enough to serve at the table of God and minister to His hunger with your worship . . . then the heavens may literally be the limit to what He will do for you and give to you. There is an amazing axiom: "The deeper you go into the palace, the fewer the people, but the greater the provision!"
Finding Favor With the King, 184

═══

SCRIPTURE READING

FIRST TIMOTHY 6:12–16, WHERE JESUS CHRIST IS DESCRIBED
AS "THE BLESSED AND ONLY POTENTATE, THE KING OF
KINGS, AND LORD OF LORDS, WHO ALONE HAS
IMMORTALITY, *DWELLING IN UNAPPROACHABLE LIGHT*,
WHOM NO MAN HAS SEEN OR CAN SEE, TO WHOM BE
HONOR AND EVERLASTING POWER."

chambers. Direct access is limited to top officials and family members— and sometimes to family alone.

God welcomes you into His presence, but first you must learn the protocol of His presence. Above all, learn to honor Him before you ask Him! The more you put Him first, the deeper He draws you into His presence and the greater the privileges and provision you receive there!

===

PRAYER

Father, thank You for the privilege of calling you Abba, Daddy. *I honor and reverence You as the Father of Lights and the Almighty One! But it is my greatest privilege to call you Father, Beloved One, Daddy. In Your presence, my every need is already met.*

PERSONAL REFLECTIONS

===

M uch of the time it seems that we take our intimate relationship with Jesus Christ for granted. The truth is, we probably have *no idea* of the power of the One with whom we are dealing! If King Xerxes was powerful, imagine the unlimited power and authority of the King of Kings!

Most Americans have little understanding of the honor, respect, and awe expected to be shown toward monarchs. That may be fine in the earthly realm (if you don't plan to travel or do business in a monarchy), but it can become a crippling deficit in the kingdom of God. We tend to underestimate the holiness and undervalue the honor due to "the blessed and only Potentate" who dwells "in unapproachable light."

"The protocol of the King's presence teaches us to honor Him before we ask Him! Don't talk to God about your need; instead, pour your love upon Him until you get to the place of worship and intimacy" (184).

The "Ninth Protocol of the Palace" says: "The deeper you go into the palace, the fewer the people, but the greater the provision!" To understand this truth, think of what it would take to see the Queen of England.

First, you must contend with the guards at the gate of Buckingham Palace. Second, you must prove that you have a legitimate reason to see the queen and seek formal permission to see her. If you make it that far, you must still wait in line until she decides to give you an audience.

Members of the royal family may legitimately *bypass* the barriers of protocol. They use private entrances, are saluted by the royal guards, are greeted by the queen's staff, and are advanced to the head of her visitor list. She may even dismiss heads of state from other nations to see family members.

Millions photograph the Royal Guards. Perhaps a thousand make it through the gates into the royal residence, and even fewer enter the inner

Day Eighty-Five

WHAT A DIFFERENCE
A DAY MAKES!

On the night before, the king had paced restlessly through
his royal residence, and finally he called for his best
sleeping aid, the royal records. Haman had returned home
from Queen Esther's first banquet to rehearse his glories to
family and friends and to bitterly plot his revenge on
Mordecai the Jew that very same night.
As for Queen Esther, perhaps she had made her early
preparations for the king and then went to sleep.
Finding Favor With the King, 188

———

SCRIPTURE READING

LUKE 12:31–32 (NASB), WHERE JESUS URGES US TO SEEK HIS
KINGDOM AND ADDS, "DO NOT BE AFRAID, LITTLE FLOCK,
FOR YOUR FATHER HAS CHOSEN GLADLY TO GIVE YOU
THE KINGDOM."

———

W hat a difference a day makes!
Long ago the prophet Isaiah prophesied of a nation "made
in a day," speaking of God's chosen people, the Jews:

"Who has heard such a thing? Who has seen such things? Shall the earth be made to give birth in one day? Or shall a nation be born at once? For as soon as Zion was in labor, she gave birth to her children."[1]

For thousands of years critics, liberal Bible scholars, and theologians scoffed at any literal interpretation of Isaiah's prediction about a nation being born in a day—especially if that nation involved the descendants of Abraham and the Arab-occupied land called "Palestine."

The millions of Jews who endured the horror of the Holocaust during World War II had no "homeland" or place of refuge at the time; they could call no nation on earth "home." They were wanderers and pilgrims scattered across the globe until everything changed *in a day*.

On May 14, 1948, the Jews declared independence for Israel as a nation for the first time in 2,900 years. *On that day,* a nation was born in a day, exactly as Isaiah predicted approximately seven hundred years before Christ's birth. What a difference a day makes!

Peter understood this too. One day and all that night, he wrestled with dark clouds of depression, sorrow, and hopelessness the only way he knew how—he went fishing. But the next day dawned with the unfamiliar sight of a man signaling them from the beach. He urged them to cast their nets one more time, and they did it—reluctantly.

When the nets came up so full of fish that they nearly sank their boats, Peter knew his life had changed *again*. The man on the shore was Jesus—resurrected from the dead and still bearing the scars of His crucifixion.[2] Just one day makes all the difference!

Are you facing a steady deluge of negative circumstances, impossible obstacles, and seemingly endless disappointments? Never give up! You serve a God who really does work the night shift! And remember that when God is at the center of your life, it only takes one day to make all the difference!

---

[1] Isaiah 66:8.
[2] See John 21:1–13.

═══

PRAYER

Father, my thoughts seem to be dominated by negative information, dire predictions, and whispered fears about how bad things are and how bad they are likely to get. Honestly Lord, I don't know what to do, but my eyes are upon You.[3] *Esther's victory reminds me that when You are involved,* one day can make all the difference!

PERSONAL REFLECTIONS

---

[3]See 2 Chronicles 20:12.

Day Eighty-Six

WHEN YOUR ENEMY PLOTS YOUR DEMISE, YOUR KING IS PLANNING YOUR REWARD

Mordecai was receiving his own private parade! Haman is in the humiliating posture of being a servant to the man for whom he built a gallows the previous night! What a life lesson!

Finding Favor With the King, 190

SCRIPTURE READING

ESTHER 6:12–13, WHERE HAMAN, THE ENEMY OF MORDECAI AND THE JEWISH PEOPLE, RETURNS HOME IN A STATE OF MOURNING OVER HIS HUMILIATING DAY SPENT HONORING MORDECAI PUBLICLY AND LOUDLY THROUGHOUT THE CITY OF SUSA—AND ALL AT THE KING'S COMMAND.

═════

D ivine reversals are written into the destiny of anyone who puts his or her trust in God. First, the Bible says, "Yes, and all who desire to live godly in Christ Jesus will suffer persecution."[1] Second, we know that God cares for His children. The experiences of Queen Esther and Mordecai should reassure us that *no one* puts one over on God.

Haman's fatal flaw is that he discounted the God of the Jews while plotting to destroy them as a people. Perhaps he overlooked this all-important fact because he never saw the Jews in Persia worshiping wooden idols or deaf and dumb stone icons. It seems he hadn't read the ancient promise:

> Behold, He who keeps Israel shall neither slumber nor sleep. The Lord is your keeper. . . . The Lord shall preserve you from all evil; He shall preserve your soul. The Lord shall preserve your going out and your coming in from this time forth, and even forevermore.[2]

It is true: *"When your enemy plots your demise, your King is planning your reward."* The mighty Haman, vizier of Persia, had set himself against the King of Kings, and *divine reversals* entered his future—a *lot* of them.

"A peasant becomes a princess and is crowned queen.
The plot of the enemy becomes the opportunity of God.
Mordecai receives a heavenly promotion and is delivered *from* death.
Haman is subjected to a demonic demotion and is delivered *to* death" (192).

God isn't like us—He isn't limited to doing one "big thing" at a time. Even as He thwarts your enemy's plans for your demise, He is

[1] 2 Timothy 3:12.
[2] Psalm 121:4–5a, 7–8.

meticulously planning your reward—with plans to deliver it to you right in front of your astounded enemies! The psalmist of Israel said it best when he declared:

> Yea, though I walk through the valley
> of the shadow of death,
> I will fear no evil: for thou art with me;
> thy rod and thy staff they comfort me.
> *Thou preparest a table before me*
> *in the presence of mine enemies*:
> thou anointest my head with oil;
> my cup runneth over.[3]

Remember: *"Favor makes you fearful to your enemies"* (192).

═══

PRAYER

Father, I know that Your enemy has become my enemy as well. He and his cohorts continually plot destruction, damage, and disappointment for me and for Your other children. But my trust is in You. Our enemy really should know better by now—You always take care of Your family members. You are my tower, my fortress, the Rock of my salvation.

PERSONAL REFLECTIONS

---

[3]Psalm 23:4–5 KJV, emphasis mine.

Day Eighty-Seven

THE PLOT OF THE ENEMY BECOMES THE OPPORTUNITY OF GOD

God is looking *for a chance to humiliate the enemy of your destiny.*
Finding Favor With the King, 192

———

SCRIPTURE READING

GENESIS 50:20, WHERE JOSEPH TOLD HIS BROTHERS—THE
SAME MEN WHO HAD THROWN HIM IN A PIT AND
ABANDONED HIM TO TRADERS DECADES EARLIER, "YOU
MEANT EVIL AGAINST ME; BUT GOD MEANT IT FOR GOOD,
IN ORDER TO BRING IT ABOUT AS IT IS THIS DAY, TO SAVE
MANY PEOPLE ALIVE."

———

One of the amazing facets of Esther's deliverance and victory in the Persian palace is that *she used her palace protocol skills in legitimate ways to set up divine reversals.* She carefully sought the king's face and royal favor rather then merely the benefits of the king's hands. Rather than jump ahead to presumptuously present her own needs, she first met the needs of the king—in two consecutive banquets!

When the time finally came to reveal her request, she carefully communicated her request in ways that *she knew* would matter the most to her husband and king. She knew this because she had devoted her adult life to understanding, serving, and pleasing him.

How well do you know *your* King? How have you spent your life since you first met Him and joined your future to His faithfulness and promises? Have you devoted yourself to understanding, serving, and pleasing Him? If so, then you should know a great deal about what truly pleases and blesses Him!

When you live a life devoted to pleasing the King, then He aggressively seeks ways to bless you while also humiliating His enemies. These enemies just happen to be the very ones who seek most often to hassle, harass, and harm you!

When you become a Christian you are "hid in Christ," or hidden from the Accuser because you totally identify with your King. This means you come under the full protection and covering of the Lord—and that makes it very risky for the enemy of your soul to threaten you. Haman discovered this truth when he dared to threaten the Jewish people with annihilation.

Joseph, the second youngest son of Jacob, experienced betrayal fueled by jealousy and imprisonment triggered by outright deceit and wrongful accusation. Yet God elevated him from a dungeon to Egypt's second in command under Pharaoh.

When Joseph finally revealed his identity to the same brothers who betrayed and abandoned him years earlier, they were afraid he would order them killed. But Joseph put into words what every follower of Christ can declare over their negative and trying circumstances: "You meant evil against me; but God meant it for good, in order to bring it about as it is this day, to save many people alive."[1]

God is in control of every life that is surrendered to Him. This principle is reaffirmed and restated in the New Testament letter to the

---

[1] Genesis 50:20.

Romans: "And we know that all things work together for good to those who love God, to those who are the called according to His purpose."[2]

Trust God, use your worship skills to set up divine reversals in your life and the lives of those you love. Then watch God take every opportunity to humiliate the enemy while delivering and blessing you.

═══

PRAYER

Father, it doesn't really matter what the enemy is planning and scheming. If I keep worshiping and obeying You, then every plot of the enemy becomes an opportunity for You to reveal Your love and power in my life!

PERSONAL REFLECTIONS

---

[2]Romans 8:28.

Day Eighty-Eight

TRAPPED IN HIS OWN SNARE, IMPALED ON HIS OWN WORDS

"As the king's wine goblet hung suspended midway between the magnificent banqueting table and his own lips, Haman must have felt a heart-stopping dread, 'a certain fearful expectation of judgment, and fiery indignation which will devour the adversaries.'"[1]
Finding Favor With the King, 193

═══

SCRIPTURE READING

ESTHER 7:4–6, WHERE ESTHER *FINALLY* REVEALS TO THE KING THAT SHE AND HER PEOPLE HAVE BEEN MARKED FOR KILLING, SLAUGHTER, AND ANNIHILATION BY HAMAN. VERSE SIX SAYS, "HAMAN *GREW PALE WITH FRIGHT* BEFORE THE KING AND QUEEN."[2]

---

[1]Hebrews 10:27.
[2]Esther 7:6b NLT, emphasis mine.

═══

H aman was trapped, with no place to run and no place to hide. He probably went to the banquet still trembling from his incredible "bad luck" at having to honor Mordecai, his hated enemy, at the command of the king. But he had no idea what awaited him.

When this descendant of an Amalekite king dared to plot against the children of God, he instantly made himself an *enemy of God.* If he had known the Scriptures, he would have known: "A fool's mouth is his destruction, and his lips are the snare of his soul."[3] Haman was building one *big* snare with his mouth and his scheming ways.

King David penned this powerful prayer sometime after Haman's ancestor had been dispatched by Samuel the prophet of God:

For my eyes are toward Thee, O God, the Lord;
In Thee I take refuge; do not leave me defenseless.
Keep me from the jaws of the trap which they have set for me,
And from the snares of those who do iniquity.
Let the wicked fall into their own nets,
While I pass by safely.[4]

In just one day, and with one divine stroke, God delivered Mordecai, Queen Esther, and the Jews under Persia's shadow from the jaws of Haman's trap. Then He arranged for the plotter to be trapped in his own plot, the hunter to be snared in his own net of destruction.

The worst part of it all, from Haman's point of view, must have been the certain dread that flooded his mind and emotions the very moment Queen Esther said the fateful words "The adversary and enemy is this wicked Haman!"[5]

---

[3]Proverbs 18:7.
[4]Psalm 141:8–10 NASB, emphasis mine.
[5]Esther 7:6.

Most of us know from certain incidents in our childhood years what it feels like to be *caught* in the act, trapped and cornered with the evidence of wrongdoing in our hand (our mouths) with no excuse good enough to fend off the "sentence for the guilty." How could we imagine what went through this evil plotter the day God himself exposed his sin and arranged his demise?

Take courage. You do not have to sink to the level of those who plot or scheme against you—you have an Advocate, a Protector, a Champion, who constantly looks out for you.

Your enemies have become His enemies. All *you* have to do is follow hard after God and put your trust in Him!

===

PRAYER

Father, from this moment on I refuse to focus my thoughts on the words, plans, and plots of the enemy. They are only setting traps, snares, and entrapments for themselves. I've set my mind on You, and I trust You to keep me in perfect peace just as You have promised.[6]

PERSONAL REFLECTIONS

---

[6]See Isaiah 26:3.

Day Eighty-Nine

FAVOR CAN RESTORE IN A DAY WHAT WAS STOLEN OVER A LIFETIME!

*We know that with the Lord a day is as a thousand years;
then perhaps it might be said that God can pack a
thousand years' worth of favor into a single day.
Favor can restore in a day what was stolen over a lifetime
(Protocol of the Palace #11).*
Finding Favor With the King, 196

≡

SCRIPTURE READING

SECOND PETER 3:8–9, WHERE PETER THE APOSTLE URGES US
TO REMEMBER THAT "WITH THE LORD ONE DAY IS AS A
THOUSAND YEARS, AND A THOUSAND YEARS AS ONE DAY,"
AND THAT GOD IS LONG-SUFFERING AND ALWAYS
KEEPS HIS PROMISES.

Queen Esther's ancestors were captured and forcibly transplanted from their homeland to the land of their captors as slaves.

God miraculously moved Esther into a position of favor, and made "the tail" become "the head," and the enslaved people who were "beneath" were promoted to positions of power at the "head" of Persia![1]

The "second-in-command" of the Persian political realm had plotted to hang Mordecai on gallows, but in the span of a night God's hand moved Mordecai up to "second in command" and had Haman planted on the gallows.

In one day, God moved the slaves called Jews into a high position of rulers over their captors with high favor in the eyes of the Persian king (and obviously, Queen Esther).

A man who had been born blind boldly told Jewish leaders what it felt like to have divine favor *restore in a day what was stolen over a lifetime*. He knew the leaders were negative, antagonistic, and skeptical to the point of sin, but it didn't stop him. He had experienced the favor of God, and he knew he had been born to reveal "the works of God" in his body.[2] After a lifetime of living in darkness, this blind man was now seeing the light *and* proclaiming the truth—even though he could lose his freedom or his life for it.

The day King David brought the last living descendant of Jonathan to the royal palace was a day of supernatural restoration. Mephibosheth was afraid that he would be killed because that was one of the ways ancient kings used to stay on the throne; they simply eliminated all challengers, naysayers, and ambitious would-be kings.

When David was still a young man staying in King's Saul's palace, he had made a solemn covenant with Jonathan. Many years later, after

---

[1]This is a reference to Deuteronomy 28:13.
[2]John 9:3.

Jonathan had fallen in battle and David had become king, David began to search for living descendants of Jonathan.

Finally he found a son of Jonathan's named Mephibosheth and sent for him. This man discovered that the king's favor could restore in a day what had been stolen over a lifetime when he heard King David say: "Do not fear, for I will surely show you kindness for Jonathan your father's sake, and will restore to you all the land of Saul your grandfather; and you shall eat bread at my table continually."[3]

The King of glory is constantly searching for ways and opportunities to restore in a day what the enemy has stolen over the lifetimes of His children!

———

PRAYER

Father, when I enter Your presence all of the pains, struggles, and disappointments of my life seem to fade away. My trust is in You, and You are well able to restore in a day what has been stolen over my lifetime!

PERSONAL REFLECTIONS

———

[3] 2 Samuel 9:7.

Day Ninety

THE BRIDE HAS NO WORRIES WHEN THE ENEMY HAS NO SONS

Esther was not and could not *be content merely to see Haman eliminated. We must remember what we learned earlier: What you do not eradicate when you are strong will come back to attack you when you are weak.*
Finding Favor With the King, 200

═══

SCRIPTURE READING

SECOND KINGS 13:16–19, WHERE ELISHA THE PROPHET
BECAME ANGRY WITH JOASH, THE KING OF ISRAEL,
FOR NOT *FINISHING* THE COMMAND OF THE PROPHET
TO STRIKE THE GROUND WITH ARROWS.
SINCE THE KING DID A HALFWAY JOB
AND ONLY STRUCK THE GROUND THREE TIMES,
HE WOULD ONLY DEFEAT HIS ENEMIES THREE TIMES
INSTEAD OF TOTALLY ELIMINATING THE THREAT
FROM ISRAEL'S FUTURE.

N o sons equals no future. As we noted in *Finding Favor With the King*, "Haman had planted a lethal virus of hatred and genocide throughout the Persian empire. A man of hate had engineered the destruction of the Jews without knowledge or input. If they did not act, they would be destroyed even after the 'father' of the plot was dead" (200).

When Esther revealed Haman's plot to King Xerxes, he quickly authorized a second decree that empowered the Jewish people to defend themselves against anyone and everyone who threatened them with force. *Some of the first enemies to be dealt with were Haman's ten sons*, along with five hundred enemies of the Jews right in the king's palace at Susa!

When a major cancerous growth is found, doctors remove the central growth first. *Then they begin searching for any branches or colonies* that have branched off from the central growth. The Lord sometimes does the same in our lives. The central source of sin is destroyed when we receive Jesus Christ as Lord and Savior. But many times we have habits, thought patterns, weaknesses, and friendships that still have the *potential* to lead us back into sin. The Holy Spirit purposefully leads us on a campaign to root out and destroy every destructive thing that still hides or resides in our lives.

Even on an international scale, when leaders have chosen to avoid the righteous use of force in favor of appeasing and coddling clearly evil rulers, such as Adolph Hitler or Joseph Stalin, the results have been bloody and costly for millions of people. Entire nations were consumed in the evil egos of these tyrants, and it took the precious blood and sacrifice of thousands of soldiers to regain freedom from them.

The same is true in the spirit realm. God expects us to release our family members, cities, and nations from the grip of darkness. Finish the fight!

It is up to us in our day to bring closure and to destroy the lingering works of the enemy. Adopt Esther's tactics. We must use the "signet ring" of the King's name while wearing the garments of praise, worship, and righteousness. We win spiritual battles by taking up the weapons of our warfare through passionate praise and indulgent worship. (201)

How many people do you know and love who are at risk because of the schemes of the enemy? *You have the power in Christ to win their release from the enemy!* "Finish the fight, and future generations can celebrate!" (202).

≡

PRAYER

Father, now that You've brought me this far, I'm determined to finish the fight and set others free as well. Thank You for giving me the authority and the courage to see this through to total victory!

PERSONAL REFLECTIONS

Day Ninety-One

ONE NIGHT WITH THE KING CHANGES EVERYTHING!

From the first blushing glance of a young girl toward her beloved, to the passionate pursuit of a bride and groom— love is indivisible from life. The greatest lesson we may learn from Esther is simply, Fall in love with the King!
Finding Favor With the King, 203

SCRIPTURE READING

ESTHER 8:15–17, WHERE WE SEE THE VISIBLE RESULTS OF THE INVISIBLE WORKINGS OF THE GOD WHO NEVER SLEEPS OR SLUMBERS. THE JEWISH PEOPLE, NEWLY REDEEMED FROM CERTAIN DEATH, HAD "LIGHT AND GLADNESS AND JOY AND HONOR."[1]

One night with the King of Kings—or even a mere thirty seconds in His presence—can change *everything*! Even seventy or eighty years of a life badly lived—a life littered with criminal acts, foolish and

[1]Esther 8:16 NASB.

thoughtless deeds, or decades spent in absolute focus upon self and self-pleasure—can all be overturned, forgiven, and redeemed in a moment of time at the cross of Jesus Christ.

The Bible is filled from cover to cover with testimonies of lives changed and transformed by a *single encounter* with God. Only one person was perfect in that entire narrative, and the rest of the imperfect folks couldn't stand it so they *killed* Him! (I'm speaking of Jesus, of course.)

The King is the key to everything in life! If you have the favor of the King, then you have everything. It doesn't matter whether you face challenges at work, in your marriage, in your physical health, or with your children. The secret to victory is still the same: *Fall in love with the King!*

> When we worship Him, the King moves heaven and earth to reverse the judgments, plots, and schemes against us, resulting in our heavenly promotion, while bringing down our true enemy (Satan) in demonic demotion. Amazingly, the Scriptures end with the Bride being caught *up*, while Satan is cast *down*!
>
> No matter who you are, what you face, or how overwhelming your circumstance may seem, do what Esther did: "She waged a wise war of worship, ultimately *finding favor with the king!*" (203)

Just remember that what your enemy meant for destruction, God meant for liberation. He is a redeeming, restoring, healing, reconciling, loving God who is *for* you and not *against* you.

When you come face to face with a battle you never asked for and hoped to avoid, don't rush around and scramble for solutions in your own strength. Go straight into the King's inner chambers; trust in your favor based on the intimate relationship Jesus gave you as a child of the · King. Worship your King, serve Him and honor Him *more* than you give place to your problem. You don't have to shout your demands from the outer gates.

> Once you've learned the protocol of His presence, once you've mastered the art of preparation, you can whisper your wishes from the intimate embrace of worship instead of announcing your

requests in formal petition from the outer courts. (204)

Never underestimate the potential of one worship encounter! Remember the Twelfth Protocol of the Palace: *One night with the King changes everything!*

———

PRAYER

Father, I've already learned the lesson of Esther—I've fallen in love with my King! One encounter has changed my destiny for eternity, and my life is in Your hands. Just one brief moment in Your presence has given me the privilege to spend eternity gazing upon Your face. Now everything has changed!

PERSONAL REFLECTIONS

GODCHASERS INTERNATIONAL MINISTRY SCHOOL

...PASSIONATELY PURSUING THE PRESENCE OF GOD

Are you hungry for hands-on training from leaders who are passionate about discipleship? Are you passionate about His presence? If so, this is the school for you. Our program offers a variety of experiences with 5 tracks of ministry to choose from: ▽**Worship,** ▽**Pastoral,** ▽**Youth,** ▽**Childrens and** ▽**Missions Ministries.** We offer advanced training through personal mentoring with a Bible-based foundation. **Student Life**...GodChasers student life hosts numerous events during the semester to bring students, faculty, and staff together.

WHAT YOU CAN EXPECT FROM THE GODCHASERS INTERNATIONAL MINISTRY SCHOOL:

1. Mentoring Environment

2. Practical Hands-on Ministry

3. Solid Biblical Foundation

4. Opportunity to Minister in Corporate Settings

5. Equipping Passionate Worshippers

6. Spiritual Training Ground That Releases the Gifts of the Spirit

7. Equipping that will Launch You Into Your Future

8. A Place of Destiny and Excitement

VISIT OUR WEBSITE TO FIND OUT MORE
www.godchasers.net/ministryschool

Our vision is to leave a spiritual legacy of passionate young men and women. We want to fuel their passion and impart to them the lessons we have learned. "My deepest desire is to launch the next generation of GodChasers and see them passionately pursuing God's presence."

Tommy & Jeannie Tenney

Tommy and Jeannie Tenney
GodChasers.network

GodChasers Ministry School is calling to those who will lay down their lives and pick up their mantle. Our mandate is to reach the earth with the gospel. Our deep passion for Jesus will bring that to pass.

Keith + Darla Collins

Keith and Darla Collins
GCIMS President/Administrator

WHAT ARE YOU WAITING FOR?

LAUNCH INTO YOUR DESTINY

P.O. BOX 3355
PINEVILLE, LA 71361 USA
Ph: 318-442-4273 ~ Fax: 318-487-6856
email: admissionsinfo@godchasers.net ~ www.godchasers.net/ministryschool

More from
Tommy Tenney

Finding Favor with the King
"On that night...." Esther 6:1
Have you ever needed a that night? Or a that day? A point in time before which things were going wrong, but after which, things began to go right? What are the ingredients to a that night? What is mixed into the recipe? Understanding what goes into creating that moment of divine favor was Esther's ultimate secret.

She learned how to find favor with the King. You can, too.

Hadassah
With Mark Andrew Olsen
Full of political intrigue and suspense, this historically accurate novel, layered with fresh insights, provides a fascinating twist on a pivotal time in religious history. Both a palace thriller and a Jewish woman's memoir, *Hadassah* brings the age-old story of Esther to life.

Hadassah Covenant
With Mark Andrew Olsen
After the death of her husband, Esther wonders if her life still has purpose. The answer lies in an astonishing, modern-day discovery of a history-altering truth. Picking up in the wake of *Hadassah*, *Hadassah Covenant* is the explosive continuation of Esther's legacy into modern times.